D1192439

THE
LORD'S TAVERNERS
FIFTY GREATEST

THE
LORD'S TAVERNERS
FIFTY GREATEST

The Fifty Greatest Post-War Cricketers
From Around The World

Selected by

Trevor Bailey
Richie Benaud
Colin Cowdrey
Jim Laker

Foreword by
HRH The Prince Philip, Duke of Edinburgh, KG, KT

The Contributors
Illustrations: Mike Francis, Ivan Rose, Rodger Towers, Ron Wootton
Text: Graham Tarrant
Statistics: Bill Frindall
Design: Serena Harrison

The Lord's Taverners and The Publishers gratefully acknowledge
the generous contribution of Ronald Gerard who sponsored all
the artists' materials used in the preparation of this book.

Heinemann/Quixote Press
10 Upper Grosvenor Street, London W1X 9PA
London Melbourne Toronto Johannesburg Auckland

First published 1983
SBN 434 98039 0
Limited Edition 434 98040 4

Introduction copyright © Trevor Bailey 1983
Text copyright © Graham Tarrant 1983
Illustrations copyright © Mike Francis 1983
(Denis Compton, Clyde Walcott, Bert Sutcliffe, Garfield Sobers, Glenn Turner, Ray
Lindwall, Barry Richards, Bishan Bedi, 'Vinoo' Mankad)
© Ivan Rose 1983
(Fred Trueman, Len Hutton, Ian Botham, Geoffrey Boycott, Brian Statham, Neil
Harvey, Don Bradman, Everton Weekes, Joel Garner, Hugh Tayfield, Kapil Dev,
Hanif Mohammad)
© Rodger Towers 1983
(Derek Underwood, Ken Barrington, Peter May, Alan Knott, Alec Bedser, Godfrey
Evans, Lance Gibbs, Frank Worrell, Vivian Richards, Rohan Kanhai, Clive Lloyd,
Richard Hadlee, Rodney Marsh, Alan Davidson, Zaheer Abbas, Imran Khan)
© Ron Wootton 1983
(Ted Dexter, Andy Roberts, Wesley Hall, Wally Grout, Keith Miller, Dennis Lillee,
Greg Chappell, Ian Chappell, Graham McKenzie, Arthur Morris, Graeme Pollock,
Mike Procter, Sunil Gavaskar)

Colour origination by Imago Publishing Limited
Typeset by Tradespools Ltd, Frome, Somerset
Printed in Spain by Mateu Cromo Artes Graficas, S.A.

WHO ARE THE LORD'S TAVERNERS?

They have been loosely described as a group of cricketing actors or acting cricketers! The Lord's Taverners are, in fact, both club and registered charity. Club Membership encompasses famous names from the world of entertainment and sport, as well as businessmen prominent in their profession. From small beginnings in 1950, we are hoping to raise half a million this year for our charitable objectives. These are:

> 'To enable youngsters to keep physically fit and mentally alert through the playing of team games, principally cricket.'

> 'To raise money for Adventure Playgrounds for under-privileged children through the auspices of the National Playing Fields Association.'

> 'To provide "New Horizon" minibuses for the mentally and physically handicapped to enable them to get away from the confines of homes or hospitals.'

The idea of *The Fifty Greatest* was conceived in my office when Ron Wootton showed me a similar book published in America of baseball stars. I am indebted to Heinemann/Quixote for having sufficient faith in the concept to agree to publish. I am also grateful to the artists and the editor who have given selflessly of their time for the Charity. Also, the selectors who have nailed their colours to the mast and are now ready to be shot at!

Finally, our thanks to our Patron and 'Twelfth Man' HRH Prince Philip, the Duke of Edinburgh for graciously consenting to write the foreword. I am confident that this unique cricket book will raise a lot of money for our Charity.

Anthony Swainson OBE
Director
July 1983

CONTENTS

The four selectors, the four artists and the editor have combined to produce a fascinating book. I do not expect everyone would agree with the selectors but that is a hazard all selectors have to face. I daresay some readers will not find all the pictures to their liking but they certainly have more character than any photograph. Of course the best part about this book is that all concerned have given their time and talents for free so that the Lord's Taverners can collect what I have every reason to believe will be a handsome profit for their charity.

1983

INTRODUCTION

One day last year I chanced to walk into The Lord's Taverners' office and Tony Swainson asked me what I thought about a new Taverners' cricket book. My initial reaction was not too enthusiastic as the market was over-crowded, until Tony came up with the idea of painted pictures of great players, not photographs. This approach had not been attempted for some time and had obvious possibilities.

We then discussed the book in outline and came down in favour of only having post-war cricketers, which raised two problems. First, which players should be included, secondly, who should make what were bound to be controversial decisions?

I have noticed that Tony possesses a mind which can be positively Machiavellian, and which enables him to persuade some poor unsuspecting innocent to take over the responsibility for a project without realising that he has volunteered, been accepted, and what is involved. On this occasion he cunningly suggested that *I* might like to choose the greatest post-war players, which, apart from anything else, was bound to be too personalised.

Without thinking I said: 'What is really needed, Tony, is a Selection Committee of Lord's Taverners who have all seen and played against the very best.' Within a few minutes I discovered myself as Chairman of a four-man Selection Committee which I had to find and then cajole into accepting.

I required three eminent Lord's Taverners, who had been distinguished Test cricketers in their own right, had subsequently seen plenty of international cricket and were willing, enthusiastic and accessible. I approached three: an England captain, a great batsman and the first man to play in over 100 Tests; an Australian captain, unquestionably one of their finest and a world-class all-rounder; and probably the finest off-break bowler in the history of the game: Colin Cowdrey, Richie Benaud and Jim Laker. They all accepted immediately, because the proceeds would be going to The Lord's Taverners. Quite apart from not having to look any further, I do not believe I could possibly have chosen better.

Our initial selection meeting took place at a splendid dinner at the Plough and Harrow during the Edgbaston Test. The most surprising feature was the number of players we all automatically chose. In fact, we had no difficulty whatsoever selecting our top sixty post-war cricketers. What took the time and the effort was reducing the number to fifty. This has inevitably meant that we have been forced to leave out some really outstanding players whom we all wanted to include. It even meant that Richie, Jim and myself had a quick and enjoyable 'get-together' in Australia last winter to settle those last few places.

The big difficulty in estimating the ability of cricketers over what is nearly a forty-year period is that the value of both runs and wickets must to some degree depend upon the quality of the opposition.

A high quality batsman selected to play in six Test matches against Sri Lanka at the present time should score heavily, and probably make twice as many runs as he would expect to do against West Indies. The World Series obviously cheapened the value of performances in the Tests played then, because most of the best players were absent. Although Peter Parfitt was a fine batsman, the four centuries he made against Pakistan might be said to flatter his Test average a little. And so on.

Some things in cricket never change. Over a period of time good batsmen will always score runs, and great batsmen will score vast quantities; while good bowlers will take wickets, and great bowlers will take a vast quantity. However, it also follows that the runs made and wickets captured must depend on the matches played.

The number of Tests has escalated dramatically in recent years, which means that all the Test quantity records, like appearances, runs scored and wickets taken, will automatically be broken; but this has nothing to do with quality. The fact that Vivian Richards has scored more runs than George Headley, or Geoff Boycott more than Sir Len Hutton, or that Dennis Lillee has captured more wickets than Ray Lindwall, or Ian Botham more than Alec Bedser, does not make them necessarily better players.

Conversely it might be argued that, just because I happened to do the 'double' on a number of occasions, something Ian Botham has never achieved, I was a better all-rounder, which is plainly absurd. It is now impossible for an England regular, even one as talented as Ian, to achieve the 'double', whereas in my era it was very feasible.

In short, then, the criteria of the Selection Committee have been quality and excellence, not merely quantity; which will help to explain the absence of some, though not all of the players.

Finally, I would like this opportunity of thanking Jim, Colin and Richie, not only for their assistance and support, but also for a series of pertinent 'one-line' comments on the 'fifty greatest'.

Trevor Bailey

EDITOR'S NOTE

Many works of reference have been used in researching this book, but special mention should be made of Christopher Martin-Jenkins' *The Complete Who's Who of Test Cricketers*, a splendidly comprehensive guide to the careers of those who have played at the highest level of the game; *The Wisden Book of Test Cricket 1876–77 to 1977–78*, compiled and edited by Bill Frindall, an indispensable and endlessly fascinating statistical history of matches won, lost and drawn, records made and broken; and, inevitably, the *Wisden Cricketers' Almanack*, without the assistance of which fewer cricket books would be written.

G.T.

THE SELECTORS

TREVOR EDWARD BAILEY

b. Westcliff, Essex, 3 December 1923
Cambridge University, Essex and England

An outstanding right-arm fast-medium bowler, tenacious batsman and brilliant fielder, Trevor Bailey achieved the double of 1000 runs and 100 wickets in a season eight times. He was a determined and fearless competitor who thrived on crises and rearguard actions, his stubborn performances at the crease earning him the media tag 'Barnacle'. He made his début for Essex in 1946, and in his maiden Test three years later against New Zealand at Headingley, took 6 for 118 in the first innings. His best Test bowling figures were 7 for 34 against the West Indians on a good wicket at Sabina Park in 1953–4. Of his many enduring innings with the bat, none was more valuable than his courageous 71 at Lord's against Australia in 1953, when he stood his ground for four and a quarter hours in a match-saving partnership with Willie Watson. His highest score in first-class cricket was 205 off Sussex in 1947; his best bowling analysis, also for Essex, was 10 for 90 against Lancashire in 1949. Bailey was captain of Essex from 1961–6 and club secretary from 1955–65. A shrewd and much respected observer of the game, he is a member of the BBC's 'Test Match Special' team and cricket (as well as football) correspondent of the *Financial Times*. He has written several books, among them *Sir Gary*, a biography of Garfield Sobers, *The History of Cricket*, a coaching manual entitled *Cricketers in the Making* and, most recently and in collaboration with Fred Trueman, a study of fast bowlers from *Larwood to Lillee*.

First-class career (1945–67): 28,642 runs (33.42) including 28 centuries, 2082 wickets (23.13), 425 catches
Test matches (61): 2290 runs (29.74) including one century, 132 wickets (29.21)

RICHARD BENAUD, OBE

b. Penrith, N.S.W., 6 October 1930
New South Wales and Australia

Richie Benaud ranks among the great Test captains, as well as being one of the finest all-rounders ever produced by Australia. To his considerable talents as a leg-spin and googly bowler, forcing right-hand bat and specialist close fielder, were later added tactical skills and qualities of leadership of the highest order. He first played for his State at the age of 18, and for Australia at 21. He went on to become the first player to score 2000 runs and take 200 wickets in Tests, and his final total of 248 dismissals was a record for Australia. His best Test analysis was 7 for 72 against India in 1956–7; but undoubtedly one of his finest performances came at Old Trafford in 1961, when with 6 for 70 in the second innings he brought about a dramatic England collapse to save the Ashes for Australia. His feats with the bat include a Test century in 78 minutes against the West Indians in 1955, and an extraordinary innings of 135 against T. N. Pearce's XI at Scarborough in 1953, which contained eleven sixes and nine fours. As a remarkably successful captain of Australia from 1958–63, he led his country in six series, winning five and drawing one. Now a journalist and television commentator for the BBC in England and Channel 9 in Australia, Richie Benaud was one of the principal advisors on the formation of World Series Cricket. His books include: *Way of Cricket*, *Tale of Two Tests*, *Spin Me a Spinner* and *Willow Pattern*.

First-class career (1948–68): 11,719 runs (36.50) including 23 centuries, 945 wickets (24.73), 255 catches
Test matches (63): 2201 runs (24.45) including 3 centuries, 248 wickets (27.03)

Ron Wootton

Ivan Rose

THE SELECTORS

MICHAEL COLIN COWDREY, CBE

b. Ootacamund, India, 24 December 1932

Oxford University, Kent and England

Colin Cowdrey has played in more Test matches than any other cricketer. A right-hand batsman and elegant stroke-maker of the highest class, he scored centuries against every other Test-playing country of his time and topped 1000 runs in a home season on 21 occasions. A useful leg-spinner in his early days, he was also a magnificent slip fielder and holds the world record for the most catches in Tests (120). He made his first-class début for Kent in 1950 and led the county from 1957–71, equalling Lord Harris' record of fifteen years as captain. His maiden Test was against Australia at Brisbane in 1954–5, and he made his last Test outing against them twenty years later on what was his sixth tour of the country. It was against Australia, too, that he recorded his hundredth Test appearance – the first player in the history of the game to do so – celebrating the event in true Cowdrey style with a century. Colin Cowdrey captained England twenty-seven times. His highest innings in Tests was 182 off Pakistan at The Oval in 1962; in all first-class matches, 307 for MCC v. South Australia at Adelaide in 1962–3. Since his retirement from full-time cricket in 1975, he has continued to be an active supporter of the game behind the scenes, serving on a number of MCC and TCCB committees. He is on the editorial board of *The Cricketer* magazine and has written four books: *Cricket Today, Time for Reflection, The Incomparable Game* and *MCC: The Autobiography of a Cricketer.*

First-class career (1950–76): 42,719 runs (42.89) including 107 centuries, 65 wickets (51.21), 638 catches
Test matches (114): 7624 runs (44.06) including 22 centuries

Mike Francis

JAMES CHARLES LAKER

b. Frizinghall, Yorkshire, 9 February 1922

Surrey, Essex, Auckland and England

Jim Laker, arguably the finest off-spinner of all time, made cricketing history at Old Trafford in 1956 when he captured 19 Australian wickets for 90 runs. In what has been known ever since as 'Laker's Test', he followed up his 9 for 37 in the first innings with 10 for 53 in the second; his 46 wickets in the series costing just 9·60 runs apiece. It was the second time that summer he had taken all ten Australian wickets in an innings, having previously performed the feat (10 for 88) for Surrey in their match against the tourists. After war service in the Middle East with the RAOC, Laker joined Surrey in 1946. On his Test début against West Indies at Bridgetown in 1947–8, he took 7 for 103 in the first innings. He exceeded 100 wickets in a season eleven times, on four occasions recording a hat-trick, and with county colleague Tony Lock formed one of the great spinning partnerships of post-war cricket. His best bowling figures were 8 for 2, on a drying wicket at Bradford in the 1950 Test Trial. As a useful tail-end batsman with a very effective square cut, he also played many valuable innings for his side. Following his departure from Surrey in 1959, Laker reappeared on the first-class scene for a brief spell with Essex, before finally retiring in 1964. Off the field he has established another successful career as a BBC television commentator, cricket writer for the *Daily Express* and author of such books as *Spinning Round the World, Over To Me, One Day Cricket* and *A Spell from Laker.*

First-class career (1946–65): 1944 wickets (18.41), 7304 runs (16.60) including 2 centuries, 270 catches
Test matches (46): 193 wickets (21.24), 676 runs (14.08)

Rodger Towers

SIR DONALD GEORGE BRADMAN

b. Cootamundra, N.S.W., 27 August 1908

New South Wales, South Australia and Australia

Although Don Bradman's playing career was almost at an end when Test cricket was resumed in 1946, his performances over the following three years more than justify his inclusion in a list of post-war cricketing greats. In the five-Test series against England in 1946–7 he scored 680 runs (97.14), with centuries at Brisbane (187) and Sydney (234). A year later it was the Indian touring side who were on the receiving end: Bradman's aggregate for the series was 715 runs (178.75), including four hundreds, two of them in the Melbourne Test (132 and 127 n.o.). In 1948 he made the last of his four tours to England as captain of what many regard as the finest Australian side ever. In a one-sided series Australia won four of the five Tests, but by his own supreme standards 'The Don's' contribution was more modest than usual: 508 runs at an average of 72.57. There were centuries at Trent Bridge (138) and Headingley (173 n.o.); but in his final Test innings at The Oval the great man, doubtless overwhelmed by the occasion, was bowled by an Eric Hollies googly for nought, second ball. He was just four runs short of achieving a Test career average of 100. Bradman was the greatest run-getter of all time, dominating all bowlers to an extent that no one else has done before or since. His judgement, timing, footwork and concentration were in a class of their own, the runs flowing from his bat in all directions with a speed and certainty that drove bowlers almost to distraction. He wasn't infallible, but he was the next best thing. Of his 117 centuries in first-class cricket, thirty-one were double hundreds, five were triple, and there was one innings of 452 not out. On average, one in every three innings produced a century. At one period he scored a hundred in eight successive Tests against England in which he batted, and twice clocked 1000 runs before the end of May. In 1949 he created yet another record by becoming the first Australian cricketer to be knighted.

First-class career (1927–49): 28,067 runs (95.14) including 117 centuries, 36 wickets (37.97)
Test matches (52): 6996 runs (99.94) including 29 centuries, 2 wickets (36.00)

Although 'The Don' was in the twilight of his cricket career, he scored a chanceless century on each of the three occasions I played against him, making me distinctly thankful that I never had to bowl against him in his prime.
T.E.B.
'The Don' – head of the world's family of batsmen.
R.B.
The only batsman who gave me an inferiority complex.
J.C.L.

Ivan Rose

FREDERICK SEWARDS TRUEMAN

b. Stainton, Yorkshire, 6 February 1931

Yorkshire and England

Not all the stories that have sprung up around the legendary character of 'Fiery Fred' are true, but his achievements as one of the greatest fast bowlers of all time cannot be disputed. He was the first bowler to claim 300 Test wickets; and in a career spanning twenty years he took five or more wickets in an innings 126 times, ten or more in a match 25 times, and four hat-tricks. Trueman's aggressive temperament was supported by an immensely strong physique, with shoulders, as Len Hutton has said, 'built like a battleship'. Accelerating along a gently curving run-up, he delivered the ball with a classical sideways action. His stock ball was the outswinger, fast and late; he also bowled a mean swinging yorker. His arrival on the Test scene in 1952 was little short of sensational. In the four-match series against India he captured 29 wickets (13.31), including 8 for 31 at Old Trafford where the opposition, unused to such pace, was humiliatingly shot out for 58. After an unhappy tour of the West Indies in 1953–4, during which he fell out of favour with the authorities, Trueman was left out of the side which travelled to Australia the following year. But he could not be ignored for long, and from 1957 to 1965 was an almost automatic choice for England. Eight times during this period he took 20 or more wickets in a series; his highest tally was 34 – against the 1963 West Indians – which included figures of 11 for 152 at Lord's followed by 12 for 119 at Edgbaston. Another mighty performance was his match-winning 11 for 88 against Australia at Headingley in 1961 (in one spell of 24 balls his figures were 5 for 0). When he wasn't bowling his heart out Trueman was a useful lower order batsman with three first-class centuries to his name, and a brilliant close fielder who could also throw accurately from the boundary with either arm. Since retiring from the game, he has had a successful career as a broadcaster and raconteur. But that's another story.

First-class career (1949–69): 2304 wickets (18.29), 9231 runs (15.56) including 3 centuries
Test matches (67): 307 wickets (21.57), 981 runs (13.81)

Had the great advantage of being supremely confident of his ability to bowl out anybody, at any time, on any wicket. Originally depended largely upon pace to remove the opposition, but became a truly great fast bowler when he learned to think out, as well as blast out, batsmen.
T.E.B.

Blessed with a powerful physique and a perfect action, his competitive spirit when roused gave him the edge over other bowlers.
M.C.C.

Ivan Rose

SUNIL MANOHAR GAVASKAR

b. Bombay, India, 10 July 1949

Bombay, Somerset and India

At 5ft 4¾ins 'Sunny' Gavaskar may not look very much, but as batsmen go he is one of the giants. Only Don Bradman has scored more Test hundreds. The right-handed Gavaskar has all the attributes of a great opening batsman: an impeccable technique for playing fast bowling (though he is equally adept against spin), immense concentration, and the patience and stamina to build a large innings. Although less inclined to hook than many other top batsmen, he is not short of strokes, executing drives, pulls, cuts and glances with confidence and power. At 21, with only twelve first-class games under his belt (enough to have notched three centuries), he was selected to tour the West Indies, and in his maiden Test series totalled 774 runs at the astonishing average of 154.80; and this despite missing the first Test through injury. His centuries in the third and fourth Tests were capped by his hundred in each innings (124 and 220) in the final match at Port-of-Spain. The bubble burst in England in 1971; but on his second visit there three years later he showed his true class with a masterly 101 in the Old Trafford Test, in conditions that were perfectly suited to the experienced English seam attack. Since then the runs have kept on coming. In Australia in 1977–8 he scored a century in each of the first three Tests, and the following year against Pakistan at Karachi hit a hundred in both innings of a Test for the second time (111 and 137). Later the same season he celebrated his appointment as captain against West Indies with a towering knock of 205 at Bombay, then went on to score 107 and 182 not out in the Calcutta Test. But by common consent, Sunil Gavaskar's finest Test innings to date was played against England at The Oval in 1979, when India were set 438 to win in 500 minutes. Thanks to a flawless 221 in just over eight hours by the little man from Bombay, they came within nine runs of an historic victory.

*First-class career (1966–   ): 20,424 runs (51.70) including 65 centuries, 21 wickets (53.47)

†Test matches (85): 7385 runs (53.51) including 26 centuries, 1 wicket (173.00)

*Excluding 1982–3 season   †Excluding 1982–3 series v. West Indies

A pocket-size battleship armed with an impenetrable defence and astonishing gun power. The bigger the battle, the better the performance.
M.C.C.

Ron Wootton

THOMAS GODFREY EVANS, CBE

b. Finchley, Middlesex, 18 August 1920

Kent and England

A magnificent wicket-keeper and master showman, Godfrey Evans had an almost permanent place in the England side from 1946–59. On his day – and he had many of them, especially in Test matches – he was unrivalled anywhere in the world. Remarkably agile for a man of his stocky build, with lightning reflexes and an intuitive sense of anticipation, he pulled off some spectacular catches and stumpings, astounding batsman and bowler alike. It was a measure of Evans' supreme skill that he stood up to the wicket to all but the fastest bowling, a technique which proved particularly successful in his long partnership for England with Alec Bedser, whose late swing and fast leg-cutter he handled brilliantly. In 1959 he claimed his 1000th victim in first-class cricket, and his 219 in Tests was a record for the time. Evans brought the same exuberance to his batting as he displayed behind the stumps. Once his eye was in he rarely failed to entertain the crowd, and against India at Lord's in 1952 he missed scoring a century before lunch by just two runs. Two years earlier at Old Trafford against West Indies his hard-hitting and timely innings of 104 had been even more impressive, coming as it did off the bowling of Ramadhin and Valentine on a far from friendly pitch. But he could defend as well as attack when the situation demanded as he showed in the Adelaide Test in 1947 when, with Denis Compton going strongly at the other end, he batted responsibly for ninety-seven minutes before getting off the mark (a record for all first-class cricket). A cheeky, chatty, eternally optimistic character, the Kent wicket-keeper was one of the most popular personalities in the game. He was also scrupulously fair, never appealing for a dismissal unless he truly believed the batsman to be out and even withdrawing an appeal if he felt on reflection that he had been mistaken. Godfrey Evans was a showman with style.

First-class career (1939–69): 14,882 runs (21.22) including 7 centuries, 1060 dismissals (811 ct, 249 st), 2 wickets (122.50)

Test matches (91): 2439 runs (20.49) including 2 centuries, and 219 dismissals (173 ct, 46 st)

His vitality and natural exuberance combined with his ability made him the perfect hub for any fielding side. He took seam and spin standing up to the stumps better than any wicket-keeper I have seen.
T.E.B.

The challenge of Test cricket and the big occasion always brought out the best in him.
J.C.L.

A great showman whose act was all energy, enthusiasm and bubble. His inspiration would carry the bowlers and fieldsmen through the longest and hottest day.
M.C.C.

Rodger Towers

MICHAEL JOHN PROCTER

b. Durban, Natal, 15 September 1946

Natal, Western Province, Rhodesia, Gloucestershire and South Africa

Deprived of Test cricket for most of his career, Mike Procter has had to be content with achieving greatness at other levels of the game. In the South African Currie Cup, for Gloucestershire in the County Championship and in a variety of limited-overs competitions, his exciting all-round performances have made him a star attraction. At his peak the tall, burly, baby-faced Procter was one of the fastest and fieriest bowlers in the world, despite a highly unorthodox action. Bowling off a long intimidating run, he would deliver the ball chest-on with a vigorous whirl of his right arm, and seemingly, though not quite, off the wrong foot. When knee trouble forced him to cut down on pace, he successfully resorted to bowling off-breaks. Procter the batsman is a magnificent striker of the ball, capable of annihilating almost any bowling attack with his devastating strokeplay. He shares with Don Bradman and C. B. Fry the world record of six successive centuries, scored for Rhodesia in 1970–1. He can also claim the rare distinction of six sixes in a row – hit off the last two balls of one over and the first four of the next. He has performed the hat-trick four times in first-class cricket and once in the Benson and Hedges Cup, and twice has produced a hat-trick and a century in the same game. On fourteen occasions he has taken 10 or more wickets in a match, the most being 14 for 76 against Worcestershire in 1980. His highest score is 254 for Rhodesia against Western Province in 1970–1; his best bowling figures, also for Rhodesia, are 9 for 71 against Transvaal in 1972–3. Procter has played in only seven Tests, all against Australia (1966–7 and 1969–70), and generally fared better with the ball than with the bat: his 26 wickets (13.57) in the four Tests of the second series being a key factor in South Africa's 4–0 victory. As an outstanding captain of Gloucestershire from 1977–81, Mike Procter showed that leadership was just another thing at which he was great.

*First-class career (1965–   ): 21,622 runs (36.33) including
47 centuries, 1383 wickets (19.18)
Test matches (7): 226 runs (25.11), 41 wickets (15.02)
*Excluding 1982–3 season

A marvellous all-rounder who would have walked into any
Test team since the war.
R.B.

Ron Wootton

ISAAC VIVIAN ALEXANDER RICHARDS

b. St. John's, Antigua, 7 March 1952

Combined Islands, Somerset and West Indies

Viv Richards is known to his fellow cricketers as 'Smokin' Joe', because of his resemblance to former world heavyweight boxing champion Joe Frazier. And like his nickname-sake, he packs quite a wallop. One of the finest West Indian batsmen of all time, the Antiguan-born right-hander is an audacious and inventive stroke-maker of punishing power who comes out fighting from the very first ball of an innings. He has every orthodox stroke at his command, executing them with footwork and timing that are almost magical; but it is the unorthodox shots, like pulling outswingers to the mid-wicket boundary or stepping wide of the leg stump to crash the ball through a vacant hole in the covers, that make the bowlers despair. Richards, who is also a very capable off-spinner and a fine fielder anywhere, made his first-class début for the Leeward Islands in 1971–2. Two years later he joined Somerset. He began his Test career – against India in 1974–5 – with innings of 4 and 3, but made up for it in his second Test at Delhi with a magnificent knock of 192 not out. During eight months in 1976 he scored 1710 runs (90.00) in Tests, a record for a calendar year. Starting off with a century (101) against Australia and missing another by just two runs, he returned home to take three more (142, 130, 177) off the visiting Indians. Then it was on to England where in four Tests (he missed a fifth through illness) he totalled 829 runs (118.42), including 232 at Trent Bridge, 135 at Old Trafford, and 291 off 386 balls at The Oval. His aggregate was the fourth highest ever for a Test series and a record for West Indies. In 1979 he helped his team to retain the Prudential World Cup with an undefeated 138 in the final, and later in the season contributed to Somerset's victory in the Gillette Cup with a typically dynamic 117. In both games he was voted 'Man of the Match'. Which is why for so many cricket fans 'Smokin' Joe' is simply 'The Greatest'.

*First-class career (1972–   ): 21,099 runs (48.95) including 63 centuries, 123 wickets (42.10)
†Test matches (47): 4129 runs (58.98) including 13 centuries, 13 wickets (54.07)

*Excluding 1982–3 season   †Excluding 1982–3 series v. India

A smiling genius and destroyer of bowling attacks everywhere. His skill and happy disposition combine to give enormous pleasure to fellow players and spectators alike, and as with many of the great cricketers he is so often at his best on the big occasion.
M.C.C.

Rodger Towers

RAYMOND RUSSELL LINDWALL, MBE

b. Mascot, Sydney, N.S.W., 3 October 1921

New South Wales, Queensland and Australia

As a boy during the 'bodyline' series of 1932–3, Ray Lindwall sat on the Hill at Sydney and watched Harold Larwood bowling. Fifteen years later he helped Australia to get its own back. It was more than sheer speed that made Lindwall such a great fast bowler. The batsman would come under a blistering barrage of in-dippers, outswingers, swinging yorkers and chest-high bumpers, all skilfully disguised and delivered at varying speeds of up to 90 mph. Just under six feet tall and athletically built, he had a perfectly balanced, accelerating run-up and a model action. His legendary partnership with Keith Miller was forged in the 1946–7 series against England, and for the next ten years, with Lindwall as the senior partner, they kept up their furious assault on batsmen around the world. On the 1948 tour of England, the demon Lindwall electrified the crowds and gave the English batsmen a few shocks as well. He captured 27 wickets (19.62) in the series, and in the last Test at The Oval destroyed a batting line-up that included Hutton, Edrich and Compton with 6 for 20 in 16.1 overs; England's total of 52 being their lowest of the century. The heavy atmosphere in England suited his bowling, and on his return there in 1953 he collected another 26 wickets (18.84) in the five Tests. Other countries got off no more lightly. Twice he took seven wickets in an innings against India; and in 1951–2 his 21 wickets (23.04) against a powerful West Indian side which included the 'Three Ws' largely contributed to their defeat in the rubber 4–1. Lindwall was the first genuinely fast bowler to reach the milestone of 200 Test wickets, and he took five or more in an innings twelve times. He was no novice either when it came to scoring runs, as his two Test hundreds show. Indeed who knows, if it hadn't been for Larwood's bowling, Ray Lindwall might easily have made his name as a batsman.

First-class career (1941–62): 794 wickets (21.35), 5042 runs (21.82) including 5 centuries
Test matches (61): 228 wickets (23.03), 1502 runs (21.15) including 2 centuries

Swung the ball in the air, both away from and into the bat, more than any other fast bowler. In addition he possessed exceptional control, a deadly yorker and a very cleverly camouflaged bouncer and slower ball.
T.E.B.
Perfection all the way along the line.
J.C.L.

Mike Francis

KENNETH FRANK BARRINGTON

b. Reading, Berkshire, 24 November 1930
d. Bridgetown, Barbados, 14 March 1981

Surrey and England

Ken Barrington, whose granite-like features wouldn't have looked out of place on Mount Rushmore, was in the best tradition of professional cricketers: reliable, determined, courageous, always putting the interests of the team ahead of his own. He joined Surrey at the age of 17 as a leg-break bowler (a talent he never lost), but quickly developed into an attacking batsman with an impressive array of strokes. After a false start to his Test career against South Africa in 1955, he was ignored by the selectors for four years; but from 1959 until his premature retirement from first-class cricket nine years later, after suffering a mild heart attack while playing in Australia, he was the anchor man of the English batting and often their only hope in a crisis. Barrington adapted to the role by abandoning his naturally aggressive strokeplay for a mainly defensive posture, for which he was sometimes ungratefully criticised and once actually dropped from the Test side. Only occasionally did he cut loose – as in his magnificent knock of 115 at Melbourne in 1966 – to show anything of his former self; though he does have the unlikely distinction of four times having reached a Test hundred with a six. A prolific accumulator of runs both at home and abroad, he scored centuries against every Test-playing country, his first two hundreds coming in consecutive Tests in the West Indies in 1959–60. His highest-ever innings was 256 against Australia at Old Trafford in 1964. Only Boycott, Cowdrey, Hammond and Hutton have scored more runs in total for England, and only Herbert Sutcliffe among the top batsmen has a better Test average. Ken Barrington died suddenly in 1981 while acting as assistant manager to the England side in the West Indies. The late Wally Grout once said of him: 'Whenever I saw Ken coming to the wicket, I thought a Union Jack was trailing behind him.' It is a fitting epitaph.

First-class career (1953–68): 31,714 runs (45.63) including 76 centuries, 273 wickets (32.61)
Test matches (82): 6806 runs (58.67) including 20 centuries, 29 wickets (44.82)

His concentration was such that when facing slow bowlers, he would actually watch the ball spinning in the air and play it accordingly.
J.C.L.

Rodger Towers

LANCELOT RICHARD GIBBS

b. Georgetown, Guyana, 29 September 1934

Guyana, Warwickshire, South Australia and West Indies

Lance Gibbs' career changed direction when his bowling did. Having started out as a leg-spinner, he switched to off-spin in his early playing days for Guyana and never looked back. Only Dennis Lillee has overtaken his record number of Test wickets (his other Test record of 27,115 deliveries is likely to remain intact for some time). Gibbs' long fingers and high arm action combined to give him exceptional spin and bounce, his skilful variations in pace ranging from slow to a brisk medium. He was later to add to his repertoire, with good effect, the ball which drifts away from the right-hander. His chest-on method of delivery and follow-through made him an outstanding fielder to his own bowling (when it was someone else's turn with the ball, there were few better catchers in the gully). For over a decade he was the spinning arm of the West Indian attack, taking five or more wickets in a Test innings no less than eighteen times, and twenty or more in a series seven times. He made his Test début against Pakistan in 1957–8, heading the averages with 17 wickets (23.05). Against Australia at Sydney in 1960–1 he took three wickets in four balls, following it up with a hat-trick in the next Test at Adelaide. In England in 1963 his 26 wickets (21.30) in the series included match figures of 11 for 157 at Old Trafford. But his best Test performance was 8 for 38 against India at Bridgetown in 1962, all eight wickets falling for just six runs in an amazing spell of 15.3 overs, fourteen of them maidens. In the course of thirteen overseas tours and eight home series Gibbs displayed remarkable consistency and stamina, despite the frequent handicap of a very sore spinning finger, now a permanently deformed reminder of his marathon bowling stints. From 1968 to 1973 he was a popular addition to the Warwickshire side, achieving career-best figures of 8 for 37 against Glamorgan in 1970. It was well worth changing direction for.

First-class career (1953–76): 1024 wickets (27.22), 1729 runs (8.55)
Test matches (79): 309 wickets (29.09), 488 runs (6.97)

One look at his right forefinger tells you why he was the biggest spinner of the ball in his time.
J.C.L.

Rodger Towers

HANIF MOHAMMAD

b. Junagadh, India, 21 December 1934

Karachi, Pakistan International Airlines and Pakistan

To say that Hanif Mohammad sold his wicket dearly is like saying that Fort Knox is difficult to get into. Few batsmen in the history of the game have possessed such a well-organised defence or been able to summon up such powers of concentration. He holds the record not only for the highest score in first-class cricket (499 for Karachi v. Bahawalpur in 1958–9: he was run out going for his 500th run in the last over) but also for the longest innings (337 in 16 hours 10 minutes for Pakistan v. West Indies in 1957–8). His record-breaking knock against the West Indians came after Pakistan had trailed by 473 on the first innings with three and a half days left to play. Thanks to his time-consuming efforts, the first match between the two countries ended in an honourable draw. A diminutive figure at the crease, he was nevertheless a right-hand opening batsman of immense stature. He would build an innings slowly, scoring many runs behind the wicket with deflections and cuts, anything short being hooked or pulled powerfully to leg. Hanif, three of whose brothers – Wazir, Mushtaq and Sadiq – also played for Pakistan, began his international career in 1952–3 against India at the tender age of 17 years 300 days. His first Test hundred (142) came two years later, also against India, and he went on to take centuries off every other country (except South Africa against whom he never played) before retiring from international cricket in 1969. He captained Pakistan in eleven of his fifty-five Tests. A Hanif innings was rarely a hurried affair. In the second Test at Dacca against England in 1961–2, he collected a century in each innings (111 and 104), batting a total of nearly fifteen hours. At Lord's in 1967, he took nine hours to score an unbeaten 187. His marathon knocks sometimes frustrated the spectators as much as the bowlers, but his batting was the rock on which Pakistan Test cricket was built. Not for nothing was he called the 'Little Master'.

First-class career (1951–75): 17,059 runs (52.32) including 55 centuries, 53 wickets (28.58)
Test matches (55): 3915 runs (43.98) including 12 centuries, 1 wicket (95.00)

The diminutive master with a rock-like defence, and an even more remarkable concentration and passion for making runs.
T.E.B.

A perfectionist who was never satisfied unless everything was properly balanced and poised. Sometimes even runs took second place to his artistry.
M.C.C.

Ivan Rose

KEITH ROSS MILLER, MBE

b. Sunshine, Melbourne, Victoria, 28 November 1919

Victoria, New South Wales, Nottinghamshire and Australia

All-rounder Keith Miller was the stuff of which heroes are made. Tall and handsome, an ex-wartime pilot whose twin passions off the cricket field were gambling and classical music, he excelled in every department of the game without ever losing his cavalier approach to it. Unpredictable, flamboyant, aggressive, but full of good humour, there was seldom a dull moment when he was in action. He was an attacking batsman in the grand style, imperiously driving all bowlers off the front foot or square-cutting the ball to the fence with a swashbuckling flourish of the bat. With his friend Ray Lindwall he formed one of the most hostile pace partnerships of all time. But although Miller was a genuinely fast bowler with a high natural action, capable of swinging the ball late in either direction, he was a man of many moods and would casually vary his pace (and the length of his run-up) according to how he felt at the time, throwing in the occasional leg-break, off-break or googly for good measure. In his first Test against England at Brisbane in 1946–7, he scored 79 and took 7 for 60 in the first innings, which remained his best bowling figures for Australia. He finished second in both the batting and bowling averages for the series, scoring his maiden Test hundred (141 n.o.) at Adelaide in the process. It was rare for him not to leave his mark on a game in some form or another, often indelibly, as at Sydney in 1950–1 when he dismissed the cream of England's batting with a crippling 4 for 37, then hit an unbeaten 145 to set up an Australian victory. In another great all-round performance in the West Indies in 1954–5, he scored three centuries and took 20 wickets in the series. His best-ever bowling figures were 7 for 12 for N.S.W. against South Australia in 1955–6; his highest score 281 not out off Leicestershire in 1956, one of seven double hundreds. But as the laconic Miller would probably say, who's counting?

First-class career (1937–59): 14,183 runs (48.90) including 41 centuries, 497 wickets (22.30)
Test matches (55): 2,958 runs (36.97) including 7 centuries, 170 wickets (22.97)

A born entertainer, whether batting, bowling or fielding, because not only was he always liable to do the unexpected and spectacular, but he also possessed good looks, physique and glamour.
T.E.B.

A golden all-rounder appropriately named after two of Australia's pre-war heroes, the aviators Keith Smith and Ross Smith.
R.B.

Ron Wootton

RONALD · J · WOOTTON

EVERTON DE COURCY WEEKES, OBE

b. Bridgetown, Barbados, 26 February 1925

Barbados and West Indies

The odds against three of the world's greatest cricketers being born within a mile and eighteen months of each other on a small Caribbean island are high enough. That they should also share the same initial and follow one another in the batting order almost defies speculation. Yet such was the case with Weekes, Worrell and Walcott: the 'Three Ws'. Along with the other members of this famous Barbadian trio, Everton Weekes, a batsman of explosive power and dazzling improvisation, made his first Test appearance in 1947–8 against England. Short, thickset and quick-footed, he was the scourge of bowlers of every type, unleashing ferocious cuts and hooks against the pace men and dancing down the wicket to drive the spinners back over their heads; his ruthless pursuit of runs winning him comparison with Don Bradman, the highest praise of all. His first Test century came in the last match of the 1947–8 series. In his next four Test innings, in India, he produced scores of 128, 194, 162 and 101, creating a world record of five hundreds in successive Test innings; he missed a sixth at Madras by just ten runs. In England in 1950 he headed the batting with 2310 runs (76.95), including four double hundreds and a career-best 304 not out against Cambridge University. In New Zealand in 1955–6 his first five innings were centuries, and he scored hundreds in three of the four Tests. At home there were Test double hundreds against England (206), India (207) and almost (197) Pakistan; yet one of his greatest Test innings was small by comparison. It was at Lord's in 1957. Against the combined pace attack of Trueman, Statham and Bailey, on a brute of a wicket with the ball rearing dangerously, Weekes, despite the pain from a cracked finger bone in his right hand, hit an inspired 90 with sixteen boundaries. West Indies lost the match but Everton Weekes won the hearts of the spectators. On such occasions his was a difficult act to follow – even if your name began with 'W'.

First-class career (1944–64): 12,010 runs (55.34) including 36 centuries, 17 wickets (43.00)
Test matches (48): 4455 runs (58.61) including 15 centuries, 1 wicket (77.00)

'The Three Ws': This remarkable trio from Barbados were unquestionably the finest 3, 4 and 5 in any Test team, and yet entirely different in style and technique. Everton Weekes was a neat, compact destroyer of bowling and the most accomplished on a bad wicket; Frankie Worrell was undoubtedly the most graceful with an elegant flowing style which enabled him to caress boundaries; Clyde Walcott was the most powerful, which combined with a very high backlift meant that he hit the ball off both his front and back foot with a brutal ferocity which has seldom, if ever, been equalled.
T.E.B.

Weekes' killer instinct made him, in my view, the best of the 'Three Ws'.
J.C.L.

Ivan Rose

SIR FRANK MORTIMER MAGLINNE WORRELL

b. St. Michael, Barbados, 1 August 1924
d. in Jamaica, 13 March 1967

Barbados, Jamaica and West Indies

When Frank Worrell died of leukaemia at the age of 42 a memorial service was held in Westminster Abbey, a measure of the respect and affection which this remarkable man commanded throughout the cricketing world. Barbados-born like his fellow 'Ws', Weekes and Walcott, Worrell began his first-class career at 17 as a slow left-arm bowler. His metamorphosis into a right-hand batsman of world class was noted two years later when he hit 308 not out against Trinidad – his highest-ever score and the first of two occasions on which he shared in a partnership of over 500. A trim, stylish, unflappable batsman, he was a superb judge and timer of the ball with a classically sound technique and an armoury of elegant shots. Even when taking the bowling apart, which he often did, his batting never lost its grace or charm. Worrell made up for missing a century in his first Test by three runs – against England in 1947–8 – by scoring 131 not out in his second. In England in 1950 he topped the Test averages with 539 runs (89.93), including a spectacular 261 in five hours thirty-five minutes at Trent Bridge. Seven years later he gave a repeat performance there, this time as a makeshift opener, carrying his bat for 191. There were other memorable innings against England, Australia, India and New Zealand; also some fine bowling feats with his now fast-medium swing: among them 6 for 38 against Australia at Adelaide in 1951–2, and 7 for 70 in the Headingley Test in 1957. Worrell was the first black man to captain West Indies, and proved to be an inspiration to his side. In fifteen Tests between 1960 and 1963 he instilled in the players a new spirit of national pride and sportsmanship, lifting them to victories over England (3–1) and India (5–0), and to the historic tie with Australia at Brisbane – as a tribute to the man and his cricket the two countries now compete for the Worrell Trophy. Frank Worrell was knighted in 1964.

First-class career (1942–64): 15,025 runs (54.24) including 39 centuries, 349 wickets (29.00)
Test matches (51): 3860 runs (49.48) including 9 centuries, 69 wickets (38.72)

Rodger Towers

CLYDE LEOPOLD WALCOTT, OBE

b. Bridgetown, Barbados, 17 January 1926

Barbados, British Guiana and West Indies

Clyde Walcott took on the role of wicket-keeper at school because as a batsman he found runs hard to come by. It was a deficiency he outgrew quickly. At the age of 20 he and his former schoolmate Frank Worrell, playing for Barbados against Trinidad, shared an unbroken stand of 574 for the fourth wicket. Walcott's contribution to the record partnership was a career-best 314 not out. Six foot one and a half inches tall and weighing fifteen stone, the right-handed Barbadian made full use of his powerful physique. Few batsmen have struck the ball harder off the back foot, his sledgehammer drives and square-cuts leaving most fielders, if they were lucky, standing. Originally selected for West Indies as a wicket-keeper batsman, he became a batsman and occasional medium-pace bowler when back trouble forced an early retirement from behind the stumps. Along with Weekes and Worrell he made his Test début in 1947–8 against England. The first of his fifteen Test hundreds came in the following series against India; then in 1950 his 168 not out at Lord's, along with the mesmerising spin bowling of Ramadhin and Valentine, helped the jubilant West Indians to their maiden Test victory on English soil. In the mid-Fifties, free of his wicket-keeping responsibilities, Walcott reached the heights as a batsman. Against England in 1953–4 he scored 698 runs (87.25), including three centuries, his 220 at Bridgetown remaining his highest Test score. A year later against Australia he did even better. His five centuries in the series (827 runs: average 82.70) set up one world record, and by scoring a hundred in each innings of a Test twice in the same rubber (126 and 110 at Port-of-Spain, 155 and 110 at Kingston) he created another. Amazingly, Australia still won the series 3–0. Early on in his Test career Clyde Walcott modestly asserted that he wasn't in the same class as the other two 'Ws'. But he grew out of that, too.

First-class career (1942–64): 11,820 runs (56.55) including 40 centuries, 35 wickets (36.25)
Test matches (44): 3798 runs (56.68) including 15 centuries, 64 dismissals (53 ct, 11 st), 11 wickets (37.09)

Mike Francis

RICHARD JOHN HADLEE, MBE

b. Christchurch, New Zealand, 3 July 1951

Canterbury, Nottinghamshire, Tasmania and New Zealand

The most outstanding of the five cricketing sons of former Test captain Walter Hadlee, Richard Hadlee is unquestionably the best fast bowler ever produced by New Zealand and currently one of the finest in the world. A wiry, hard six-footer with an excellent side-on action, he bowls at a lively, hostile pace, troubling most batsmen with his sharp movement and lift. He displays the same uncompromising aggression when batting, though switching from right-arm to left-hand to do so; his sustained hitting, particularly in limited-overs cricket, justifiably earning him all-rounder status. Richard followed his brother Dayle, a fast-medium bowler, into the New Zealand team, making his début against Pakistan in 1973. For the next three years he was in and out of the side; then his breakthrough came in the third Test against India at Wellington in 1976. Coming on initially as the fourth seamer, he took 4 for 35 followed by 7 for 23 – the best match figures by a New Zealander in Tests. Since then he has been an automatic selection. In New Zealand's first-ever victory over England at Wellington in 1978, he had a match analysis of 10 for 100, including 6 for 26 in the second innings as England were shot out for 64. Two years later he turned in an impressive all-round performance in the three-Test series against the visiting West Indians. In the first Test his figures were 11 for 102, with New Zealand winning by one wicket; in the second, which was drawn, he hammered the pace attack of Holding, Roberts, Garner and Croft for 103 off 92 balls. Hadlee has taken more Test wickets than any other New Zealander, and is the only one to have achieved the Test double of 1000 runs and 100 wickets. In 1982, playing for Nottinghamshire, he topped the English first-class bowling averages for the second year running. In the previous season he had been the only bowler in the country to capture 100 wickets, paving the way for Notts to win their first County Championship for 52 years.

*First-class career (1972–   ): 5461 runs (25.75) including 6 centuries, 743 wickets (19.87)
Test matches (40): 1300 runs (21.66) including one century, 179 wickets (25.72)
*Excluding 1982–3 season

The finest all-rounder to have come out of New Zealand.
J.C.L.

Rodger Towers

ARTHUR THEODORE WALLACE GROUT

b. Mackay, Queensland, 30 March 1927
d. Brisbane, Queensland, 9 November 1968

Queensland and Australia

'Never give a sucker an even break' was a favourite expression of wicket-keeper Wally Grout. But it was a philosophy he failed to live up to at Trent Bridge in 1964 when Fred Titmus, opening the innings for England, found himself hopelessly stranded halfway down the pitch, having dashed off for a quick single and collided with bowler Neil Hawke. Grout, the ball in his hand, declined to take advantage of the situation and allowed Titmus to regain his ground. It was a typically sporting gesture from a man who, in less exceptional circumstances, let few chances go begging. His 187 dismissals in fifty-one Tests is the sixth highest total by a wicket-keeper, and he had a better strike rate than either Evans or Knott, both of whom are ahead of him on aggregate. Grout had to wait until he was 30 before getting into the Test side, but once there he made the position indisputably his own for the next ten years. Short and sturdy, and wonderfully agile, his speciality was the spectacular diving catch down the leg-side. On his international début, against South Africa at Johannesburg in 1957, he became the first wicket-keeper to claim six dismissals in a Test innings. All six were caught, four off the bowling of Alan Davidson. It was a combination that would appear on the scoresheet many times thereafter. On five other occasions he picked up five victims in a Test innings, and twice totalled eight for the match. He also holds the world record for the most dismissals in a first-class innings: eight, all caught, for Queensland against Western Australia in 1959–60. As a tenacious lower order batsman, Wally Grout played many valuable knocks for Australia and often proved to be a difficult man to dislodge in a crisis. His sudden death following a heart attack, just two years after his retirement from the game, was a stunning blow to the cricketing world.

First-class career (1946–66): 5168 runs (22.56) including 4 centuries, 587 dismissals (473 ct, 114 st)
Test matches (51): 890 runs (15.08), 187 dismissals (163 ct, 24st)

A great patriot for his beloved Australia and Queensland.
R.B.

Ron Wootton

RONALD N. WOOTTON.

DEREK LESLIE UNDERWOOD, MBE

b. Bromley, Kent, 8 June 1945

Kent and England

Until he signed on for World Series Cricket, it was a fair bet that Derek Underwood would become the leading Test wicket-taker of all time. As it is, only Lillee, Gibbs and Trueman have more to their name. Back in 1963, the 18-year-old Underwood created quite a stir when he became the youngest bowler ever to take 100 wickets in a season, his maiden season in first-class cricket. He was still only 25 when he reached the 1000 mark (only Wilfred Rhodes and George Lohmann from the 'Golden Age' had achieved the feat earlier in life). Although generally classified as a left-arm spinner, Underwood cuts rather than spins the ball, relying on clever variations of pace and angle to confound the batsman. His slow-medium pace is faster than that of most spinners, and on rain-affected wickets especially he can make the ball move and lift alarmingly. His almost painful aversion to having runs scored off him is reflected in his unflagging accuracy. He won his England cap against West Indies in 1966, but it was against Australia two years later that he really got among the Test wickets. In the last match of the series at The Oval, on a drying pitch after a thunderstorm, and in a race against time, he took 7 for 50 in 31.3 overs to win the game for England, snatching the last wicket five minutes from the end. He showed the same destructive form in 1969, taking 24 New Zealand wickets in three Tests for just over nine runs apiece. His biggest haul in a single Test match came at Lord's against Pakistan in 1974, when, once again on a wet wicket, his figures were 5 for 20 and 8 for 51. Overseas his 29 wickets (17.55) in the 1976–7 series against India, and his 7 for 113 in Australia's first innings at Adelaide in 1975 (11 for 215 in the match), must rank among his finest performances. Performances which have justly earned Derek Underwood the nickname 'Deadly'.

First-class career (1963–   ): 2118 wickets (19.81), 3990 runs (9.41)
Test matches (86): 297 wickets (25.83), 937 runs (11.56)

In a class of his own. On good wickets he has exceptional control and accuracy; on anything approaching a helpful pitch, he is a match-winner.
J.C.L.

Rodger Towers

ANDERSON MONTGOMERY EVERTON ROBERTS

b. Urlings Village, Antigua, 29 January 1951

Combined Islands, Hampshire, Leicestershire, New South Wales and West Indies

Like a professional hit man, Andy Roberts displays very little emotion when he disposes of one of his targets. A brief smile, a knowing look, and then he is ready to take out a contract on the next batsman. The first Antiguan to play for West Indies, he was at his peak an extremely fast and hostile bowler, with an explosive and well-concealed bouncer which he used sparingly but to very good effect. More recently, as his pace has slowed, he has concentrated on getting movement in the air and off the seam. He made a modest Test début against England at Barbados in 1974; but then, in a sensationally successful first season in county cricket, took 119 wickets (13.62) for Hampshire. His devastating form continued that winter in India and Pakistan, where he captured 44 wickets in seven Tests, including 12 for 121 at Madras – the first West Indian to take twelve wickets in a Test match. In Australia the following year, on what was otherwise a disappointing tour for the West Indians, he was again the most successful bowler, collecting 22 wickets (26.36) in the series and recording his best-ever Test figures of 7 for 54 at Perth. His 28 wickets (19.17) against England in 1976, ten of them for 123 at Lord's, helped his side to win the rubber 3–0. During the series Roberts picked up his hundredth wicket in only his nineteenth Test match, and in the record time of two years and 142 days (later to be shortened by Ian Botham). Along with several of his fellow West Indians he signed up for World Series Cricket in 1978, and although he has played in Test matches since, it has not been with the same dynamic impact as before. In limited-overs cricket especially, Roberts has shown himself to be a very handy performer with the bat, demonstrating that when the occasion demands, he can do a hit job on bowlers, too.

*First-class career (1970–   ): 754 wickets (20.93), 2872 runs (15.11)
†Test matches (40): 173 wickets (25.90), 610 runs (13.55)
*Excluding 1982–3 season   †Excluding 1982–3 series v. India

Pace, venom, hostility – and expressionless. Which means you never know when to expect the bouncer.
J.C.L.

Ron Wootton

RONALEN WOOTTON.

SIR LEONARD HUTTON

b. Fulneck, Yorkshire, 23 June 1916

Yorkshire and England

When Len Hutton returned to Yorkshire after the war he was six years older and his left arm two inches shorter (the result of a fall in an army gym, it was a disability he overcame as a batsman with predictable courage and skill). The youthful opener who had set a world record with his monumental 364 against Australia in 1938 was now an altogether more mature player, destined to lead England to her finest cricketing hour for twenty years. Hutton was a model batsman with an exemplary technique, tenacious and disciplined in defence, stylish and fluent in attack. Compton apart, he patently outclassed the rest of the English batting in the years after the war, constantly demonstrating his mastery over bowlers and wickets alike. Many of his greatest triumphs came out of adversity. Having shown himself to be vulnerable, like everyone else, to the hostile bumpers of Lindwall and Miller in 1948, he was dropped for one Test, only to return with a magnificent 81 at Headingley and top scores for England of 30 and 64 (out of 52 and 188) in the débâcle at The Oval. In 1950, it was Hutton who finally mastered the West Indian spinning wizards Ramadhin and Valentine with an unbeaten 202 in the last Test; and in Australia in 1950–1 he stood virtually alone as England went down 4–1, averaging 88.83 for the series. He played many memorable innings in his long career but none finer than his majestic 145 against Australia at Lord's in 1953, the year England regained the Ashes under his leadership. As England's first professional captain of modern times he proved to be a determined and effective leader. Out of twenty-three Tests, he won eleven and lost only four – and never a series. One of his most impressive performances was in the West Indies in 1953–4 when he led England to a remarkable draw in the rubber after they had lost the first two Tests, Hutton personally contributing 677 runs at an average of 96.71. He was knighted in 1956.

First-class career (1934–60): 40,140 runs (55.51) including 129 centuries, 173 wickets (29.42)
Test matches (79): 6971 runs (56.67) including 19 centuries, 3 wickets (77.33)

A master craftsman, whose style was so elegant that he was a delight to watch even when scoring slowly, while his cover drive was something to treasure long after its execution. Opening the innings with him was, for me, an honour, a pleasure and an education, while he was also a marvellous judge of a run.
T.E.B.

Truly one of the all-time greats, and had it not been for the injury to his arm, which eliminated his hook shot among other things, he would have been even greater.
J.C.L.

Ivan Rose

Ivan Rose. 83.

IAN TERRENCE BOTHAM

b. Heswall, Cheshire, 24 November 1955

Somerset and England

Had it been reported in the summer of 1981 that Ian Botham could walk on water, few English cricket supporters would have challenged the statement. In the space of three Test matches against Australia, having just been stripped of the captaincy, he led an amazing fight back by England which converted a 1–0 deficit into a 3–1 lead, with two of the victories plucked daringly from the jaws of defeat. Botham's contribution to the heart-stopping events of that summer included two storybook exhibitions of controlled hitting (149 not out at Headingley and 118 at Old Trafford) and an eleventh-hour 5 for 11 (5 for 1 in 28 balls) at Edgbaston. At his best, and when fully fit, England's resident hero takes on the aspect of a cricketing Superman: a batsman of Herculean power, a stunningly alert close fielder, and a cunning and hostile fast-medium bowler who can swing the ball prodigiously in either direction. Time after time his courage, strength and determination have combined with his extraordinary natural talent to change the course of a game, his energy and enthusiasm lifting the performance of the players around him. On his first day of Test cricket against Australia in 1977, he took 5 for 74. Since then Botham and the statisticians have had a series of field days. In 1978 against Pakistan at Lord's he became the first player in a Test to hit a century (108) and take eight wickets (8 for 34) in an innings. Two years later in the Golden Jubilee match at Bombay, he was the first to make a century (114) and take ten wickets (13 for 106) in a Test. His hundredth Test wicket came in the then record time of two years nine days, and his pulverising 208 off 226 deliveries against India at The Oval in 1982 was the fastest double hundred by an Englishman for nearly thirty years. During the 1982–3 series 'down under', he became the first cricketer to score 3000 runs and take 250 wickets in Tests, and the first since Wilfred Rhodes to complete the double of 1000 runs and 100 wickets against Australia. But that's the least one expects from Ian Botham.

First-class career (1974–   ): 9849 runs (32.29) including 20 centuries, 755 wickets (24.77)

Test matches (59): 3266 runs (36.69) including 11 centuries, 267 wickets (24.47)

A true genius who lives dangerously, but no one should ever try to curb his flamboyance. Having achieved so much so quickly, one can only hope that he will stay fit and hungry.
M.C.C.

One of the most exciting match-winning cricketers England has ever produced, and certainly our best all-rounder at international level this century. A fearsome orthodox hitter, devastating swing bowler, and outstanding all-purpose fieldsman.
T.E.B.

Ivan Rose

ROBERT GRAEME POLLOCK

b. Durban, Natal, 27 February 1944

Eastern Province, Transvaal and South Africa

Graeme Pollock was only 26 when his — and South Africa's — Test career came to an end. But by then this brilliant left-hander had already scored seven centuries in just twenty-three Tests, two of them double hundreds. In more senses than one, Pollock has always been a batsman in a hurry. He was still thirty days off his seventeenth birthday when he made a century in the Currie Cup (the youngest player ever to do so), and not yet 20 when he scored his first two Test hundreds (122 and 175) in consecutive matches against Australia in 1963–4. Well over six feet tall and powerfully built, he is a majestic striker of the ball who sets out to dominate the bowling from the word go. Equally strong off the front and back foot, he drives, pulls, cuts and hooks with strokes that bear the hallmark of genius. One of his greatest innings was against England at Trent Bridge in 1965. With the score at 43 for 4 and the humid conditions favouring the English seam bowlers, Pollock raced to 125 out of 160 in two hours twenty minutes. South Africa went on to win the match and the series. (In the same game his brother Peter took 10 for 87 with his fast bowling.) Two remarkable innings from the 1966–7 series against Australia demonstrate the South African's astonishing versatility. In the first Test at Johannesburg, he made 90 in 116 minutes with attacking shots mainly off the front foot. A week later, forced through a thigh injury to play almost entirely off the back foot, he scored 209 out of 353, the first 100 coming off 139 balls. With an innings of 105 in the fifth and final Test, he ended the series with 537 runs (76.71) to his credit. His highest score of 274, also against Australia, came in what was to be his last Test series in 1969–70. Since then Graeme Pollock has scored thousands of runs, but almost all of them, sadly, inside the boundary of his own country.

**First-class career (1960–   ): 17,534 runs (56.01) including
54 centuries, 43 wickets (47.95)*
*Test matches (23): 2256 runs (60.97) including 7 centuries, 4
wickets (51.00)*
*Excluding 1982–3 season

**Drives good length seam bowling on the up along the ground
off his front foot more violently than anybody, so that deep
extra cover becomes a more dangerous position than silly
mid-off is when a mere mortal is batting.**
T.E.B.
A tragedy his genius has been confined to his own country.
R.B.

Ron Wootton

Ruald J. Wootton.

WESLEY WINFIELD HALL

b. Bridgetown, Barbados, 12 September 1937

Barbados, Trinidad, Queensland and West Indies

The sight of Wes Hall steaming up to the wicket was enough to strike terror into the soul of any batsman. Well over six feet tall, broad shouldered, his eyes bulging belligerently and a gold cross swinging from his neck, he resembled an angry voodoo god. It wasn't all an illusion either: his delivery speed was measured at a frightening 91 mph and he once broke Peter May's middle stump clean in two. Hall's own breakthrough in Test cricket came during West Indies' tour of India and Pakistan in 1958–9. On pitches calculated to lower the spirits of most fast bowlers, he captured 46 wickets (17.76) in eight Test matches, including a hat-trick at Lahore, the first in Tests by a West Indian. In 1959, against England in the Caribbean, he was partnered for the first time by Charlie Griffiths, although it wasn't until 1963 that they became the regular opening attack for West Indies and the most fearsome pair of fast bowlers in the world. Hall was unquestionably the greater of the two, with a perfect bowling action (unlike Griffiths' which at times was decidedly suspect) backed up by an impressively strong physique. Despite his lengthy run, he was able to maintain his pace for exceptionally long spells, even in the most trying conditions. A memorable example came in the Lord's Test in 1963. On the last day Hall bowled unchanged for three hours and twenty minutes, finishing with 4 for 93 off 40 overs as the match climaxed in a nail-biting draw. Not surprisingly for a man of his size, he was no mean striker of the ball himself and on one occasion scored 102 in sixty-five minutes against Cambridge University. But it is for his marvellously aggressive bowling that he is best remembered. Despite appearances when he had the ball in his hand, he was an amiable character with a clownish sense of humour and a well-deserved reputation for being a good sport. It was something for the batsman to hang on to as Wes Hall ran in to bowl.

First-class career (1956–71): 546 wickets (26.13), 2673 runs (15.10) including one century
Test matches (48): 192 wickets (26.38), 818 runs (15.73)

His long run-up, body action and follow-through provided one of the most aesthetically exciting sights in the game. He reminded me of one of those beautiful black thoroughbred stallions he loves so much.
T.E.B.

The fastest bowler I ever faced. A chivalrous character on and off the field, when he broke my arm at Lord's in 1963 he was even more upset than I was.
M.C.C.

Ron Wootton

ROHAN WESTON

IAN MICHAEL CHAPPELL

b. Unley, Adelaide, S.A., 26 September 1943

South Australia and Australia

Part of an Australian cricketing family that includes brothers Greg and Trevor and grandfather Victor Richardson, Ian Chappell made a predictably early start to his first-class career. At 18 he was a regular member of the South Australian side and his first Test appearance, against Pakistan, came when he was only 21. An attractively aggressive right-hand batsman, useful leg-spin bowler and brilliant slip fielder, Chappell was always a tough competitor; a characteristic which came to the fore when he took over the Australian captaincy in 1971. Surprisingly for a batsman of his calibre, there was only one century (151 v. India at Melbourne in 1967–8) in his first thirty Test innings. But after a successful tour of England in 1968, when his earlier experience in the Lancashire League gave him a head start over the other young Australian batsmen on English pitches, he began to fulfil his initial promise. Back in Australia later that year he took 548 runs (68.50) off the visiting West Indians, with centuries in consecutive Tests at Brisbane (117) and Melbourne (165). Following a humiliating 4–0 defeat at the hands of South Africa, and a personally disappointing tour with the bat, Chappell was appointed captain of Australia for the final Test against Ray Illingworth's 1970–1 side. Although they lost the match, and with it the Ashes, it proved to be a turning point in Australia's fortunes. Under Chappell's shrewd and abrasive leadership, and with players like Dennis Lillee, Jeff Thomson and Greg Chappell coming through, Australia entered upon a new winning era. Pakistan, West Indies, New Zealand and, most satisfying of all, England were beaten in turn; and despite his responsibilities as captain, Chappell continued to be a prolific run-getter, notching centuries against all of them. In the Wellington Test against New Zealand in 1974 both Chappells scored hundreds in each innings, a record that is unlikely to be broken. In 1975, although he remained a valuable member of the Test side, Ian handed over the captaincy to brother Greg, thus keeping Australia's top cricketing job safely in the family.

First-class career (1961–80): 19,680 runs (48.35) including 59 centuries, 176 wickets (37.57)
Test matches (75): 5345 runs (42.42) including 14 centuries, 20 wickets (65.80)

Not as naturally gifted as his brother Greg, but I would prefer to have him coming to the crease when the going was very tough, because he had a ruthless streak which also helped to make him such an outstanding and effective captain.
T.E.B.

Australia's longest ever Test match sequence without victory ... and then came Chappell.
R.B.

Ron Wootton

RONALD J. WOOTTON.

GREGORY STEPHEN CHAPPELL, MBE

b. Unley, Adelaide, S.A., 7 August 1948

South Australia, Queensland, Somerset and Australia

Greg Chappell is a man for the big occasion. In his first Test he scored 108 against England at Perth; in his first Test as captain, against West Indies at Brisbane, he made 123 and 109 not out. Tall and straight as a guardsman, and as impeccably turned out, he has been Australia's premier run-scorer for more than a decade. He is a batsman in the master class, an elegant and commanding stroke-maker with a classical repertoire of shots, from handsome full-blooded drives to delicate cuts and glances. Not content to rest on his batting laurels, he is also a useful medium-pace swing bowler and a magnificent slip fielder. Greg followed his brother Ian into the South Australian side in 1966; then, after two formative seasons with Somerset, he joined him in the Australian team. After his distinguished Test début in 1970–1 came a successful tour of England the next year, with innings of 131 at Lord's and 113 at The Oval (Ian Chappell contributing 118 at the other end). Two years later against New Zealand the Chappell brothers surpassed themselves, both getting a century in each innings: Greg 247 not out and 133, Ian 145 and 121. Greg took over the captaincy from his brother in 1975–6, Australia thrashing West Indies 5–1 in the series with the new skipper scoring 702 runs (117.00); but, less extrovert than Ian, he has proved for the most part to be an efficient rather than an inspiring captain. After a spell with World Series Cricket he returned to lead Australia in the triangular tournament of 1979–80, taking centuries off both West Indies and England, and in the course of the next two years hit three double centuries in Tests: 235 and 201 against Pakistan, 204 off India. Having relinquished the captaincy a second time, he was recalled to lead Australia against England in 1982–3. His century at Adelaide was his twenty-second for his country, taking him into second place behind Bradman. Australia won the series 2–1 to regain the Ashes, Greg Chappell once again rising to the big occasion.

*First-class career (1966–   ): 22,786 runs (52.74) including 68 centuries, 282 wickets (28.59)
Test matches (81): 6680 runs (53.01) including 22 centuries, 47 wickets (37.36)
*Excluding 1982–3 season

He possesses a wide repertoire of strokes, including an exquisite on-drive. When in full flow for Australia, he looks like a schoolmaster playing with schoolboys.
T.E.B.

Elegance, skill and flair, as well as a great run-getter.
R.B.

Ron Wootton

MULVANTRAI HIMMATLAL ('VINOO') MANKAD

b. Jamnagar, India, 12 April 1917
d. Bombay, India, 21 August 1978

Western India, Nawanagar, Maharashtra, Gujarat, Bengal, Bombay, Rajasthan and India

At Lord's against England in 1952 'Vinoo' Mankad, opening the innings for his country, scored 72 and 184, and bowled 97 overs of leg-spin to take 5 for 231. It was a remarkable effort even by the standards of India's greatest all-rounder. A right-handed batsman, though he bowled left, his approach was essentially pragmatic. He was content to bat anywhere in the order and was quick to adapt his tactics to the state of the game. Skilful and patient in defence, he was a fine striker of the ball on the leg-side and executed a perfect cover drive. His slow left-arm bowling was orthodox in style but exceptional in quality. He spun the ball sharply and had a masterly control of flight and length. At his peak he was probably the best bowler of his type in the world. Although he had played representative cricket before the war, it was 1946 before Mankad made his Test début. On the same tour of England he became the only Indian to have achieved the 'double', scoring 1120 runs and capturing 129 wickets. It was one of many such landmarks in Mankad's career. He was the first Indian to make a Test hundred against Australia (116 at Melbourne in 1948); his magnificent bowling at Madras in 1952 — 8 for 55 and 4 for 53 — paved the way for India's first-ever Test victory over England; he ensured that Pakistan got off to a bad start in international cricket by taking a match-winning 13 for 131 in their first official Test; and in 1956 against New Zealand he established a world record opening partnership in Tests of 413 with Pankaj Roy, his own contribution 231 (having scored 223 at Bombay earlier in the series). Until Ian Botham, his was the fastest Test double of 1000 runs and 100 wickets on record, achieved in only 23 matches. Mankad captained India six times. He made his final Test appearance in 1959, leaving his son Ashok, who followed him into the Indian side, with a lot to live up to.

First-class career (1935–63): 11,544 runs (34.69) including 26 centuries, 781 wickets (24.53)
Test matches (44): 2109 runs (31.47) including 5 centuries, 162 wickets (32.32)

His performance becomes even more impressive when you consider that many of his wickets were taken on 'shirtfront' pitches in India.
J.C.L.

Mike Francis

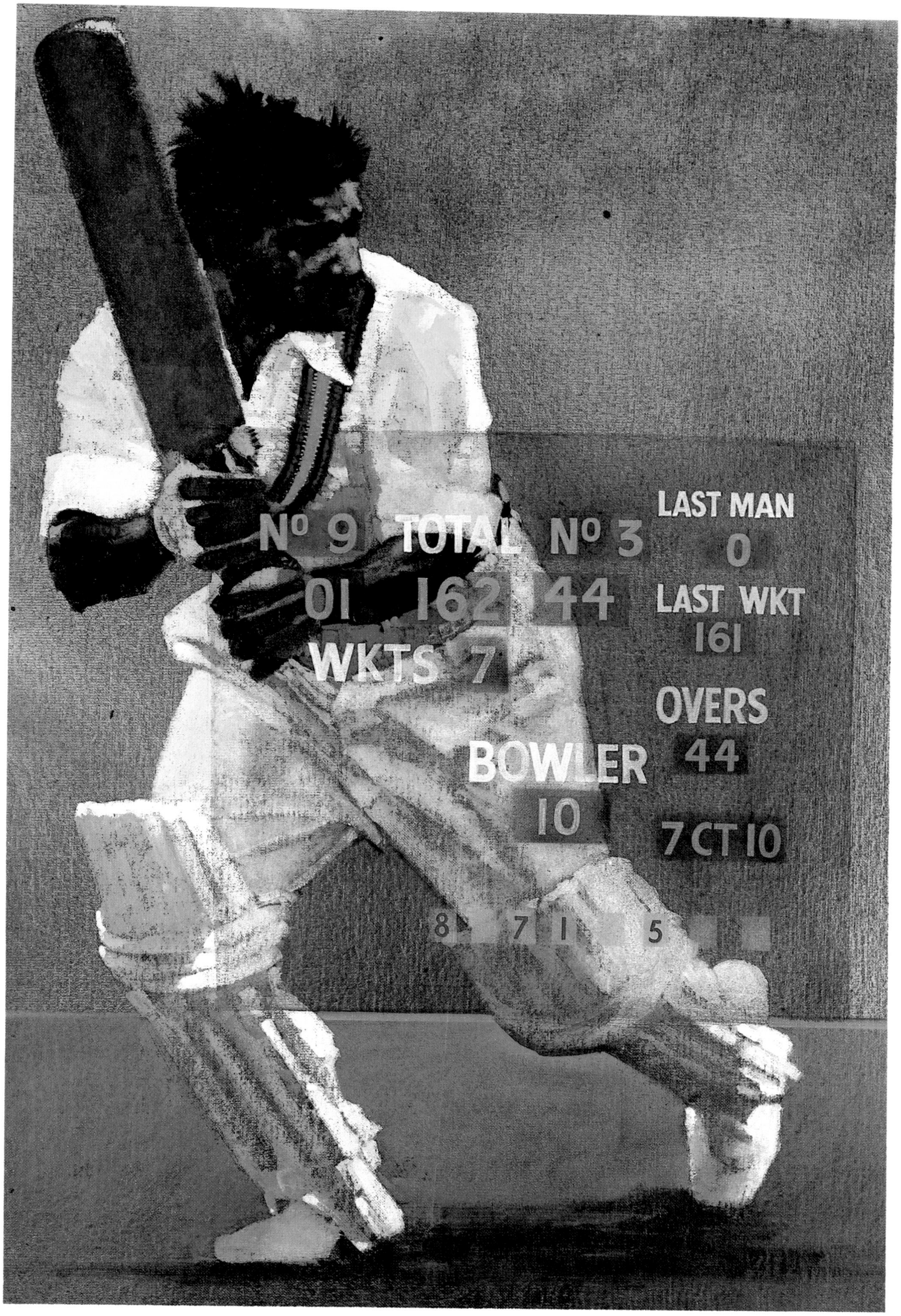
LAST MAN
Nº 9 TOTAL Nº 3
0
01 162 44
LAST WKT
161
WKTS 7
OVERS
BOWLER
44
10
7 CT 10
8 7 1 5

BERT SUTCLIFFE

b. Auckland, New Zealand, 17 November 1923

Auckland, Otago, Northern Districts and New Zealand

Bert Sutcliffe first came to the attention of the cricket world in 1947 when he scored 197 and 128 for Otago against the MCC at Dunedin. A great opening batsman and one of the finest left-handers of his generation, he was a classically correct player with a glorious range of strokes all round the wicket. His cover driving off the back foot was a particular delight to all but the opposition. In Sutcliffe's day there were limited opportunities for a New Zealander to play first-class cricket. Apart from the occasional overseas tour and the short domestic Plunket Shield competition, most cricket was at amateur club level. Nevertheless Sutcliffe managed to collect 44 first-class hundreds in his career, including seven on the 1949 tour of England when he totalled 2627 runs (59.70) in the season. He twice scored more than 300 in an innings when batting for Otago, his 385 against Canterbury in 1952–3 still remaining the highest ever by a New Zealander. With Don Taylor he shares a world record of two double century opening stands in the same match (220 and 286 for Auckland v. Canterbury in 1948–9), and on three other occasions hit a century in each innings of a game. His highest Test score was 230 not out against India at Delhi in 1955–6, a series in which he collected 611 runs at an average of 87.28. At Johannesburg in the second Test against South Africa in 1953–4, he showed that courage was another of his attributes. Struck on the head by a ball from fast bowler Neil Adcock before he had scored, he was carried off to hospital concussed but returned later, bandaged and still somewhat dazed, to hit a defiant and undefeated 80 (including seven sixes) out of 106 in 112 minutes. It came as a shock to the South African bowlers, but New Zealanders were used to great deeds from Bert Sutcliffe.

First-class career (1942–66): 17,283 runs (47.22) including 44 centuries, 86 wickets (37.95)
Test matches (42): 2727 runs (40.10) including 5 centuries, 4 wickets (86.00)

Had he been born an Englishman or played county cricket he wouldn't have been far behind his illustrious namesake.
J.C.L.

Mike Francis

DENNIS KEITH LILLEE, MBE

b. Subiaco, Perth, W.A., 18 July 1949

Western Australia and Australia

According to Dennis Lillee, the season he spent with the Lancashire League club Haslingden in 1971 was a turning point in his career. He had already won his Australian cap, taking 5 for 84 in his maiden Test against England at Adelaide a few months before, but bowling under English conditions forced him to concentrate more on line and length and movement off the pitch than on sheer speed. The lessons were well learnt. Returning to Australia that winter, he demolished the Rest of the World at Perth with 8 for 29, including one spell of 6 for 0; and back on English soil with the Australian side in 1972, he dominated the series taking 31 wickets (17.67) in the five Tests. Lillee has never concealed his dislike of batsmen, his aggression sometimes spilling over into verbal abuse. But great bowling actions speak louder than words, and in his prime Lillee's positively roared. His bouncer was full of venom and his deadly outswinger fed a constant stream of catches to the predatory Marsh and the cordon of slips alongside him. Lindwall apart, there has been no other Australian fast bowler since the war to touch him. In 1973 it seemed that his career had come to a premature end when he broke down in the West Indies with four stress fractures in the back; but with tremendous courage and determination and six weeks in plaster, he made himself fighting fit again, joining forces with Jeff Thomson a year later to destroy Mike Denness' side in Australia. Between them they captured 58 of the 108 wickets that fell to bowlers, with Lillee's share 25 (23.84). The visiting West Indians had an equally torrid time in 1975–6, Lillee this time leading the assault with 27 wickets (26.37) as they crumpled to a 5–1 defeat in the rubber; and in the Centenary Test against England at Melbourne in 1977 it was his 11 for 165 that won the match for Australia. In 1981 he showed that not even records could stand in his way when he overtook Lance Gibbs to become the greatest Test wicket-taker of all time.

First-class career (1969–　): 747 wickets (22.38), 2038 runs (14.25)
†Test matches (64): 332 wickets (23.35), 874 runs (13.65)
Excluding 1982–3 season　†Excluding Test v. Sri Lanka 1982–3

The Lillee bouncer was close to being lethal, his yorker frequently was. He remained a match-winning bowler at international level after he had lost some of his pace, because he also possessed a splendid action and exceptional control.
T.E.B.

The greatest.
R.B.

Ron Wootton

RONALD J WOOTTON.

PETER BARKER HOWARD MAY, CBE

b. Reading, Berkshire, 31 December 1929

Cambridge University, Surrey and England

Peter May is widely regarded as being the finest English batsman to have emerged since the war. His masterly technique made him equally at home against the best of pace or spin, and there has been no better performer on a sticky wicket. A commandingly tall figure at the crease, with broad shoulders and strong wrists, he was a magnificent driver of the ball on both sides of the wicket and off either the front or back foot; his on-driving especially was second to none. May was the most outstanding of the crop of brilliant young batsmen produced by the Universities in the late Forties and early Fifties. At the age of 21 he joined the exclusive ranks of those who have scored a century in their first Test, with an innings of 138 against South Africa at Headingley. His career faltered slightly in 1953 after a fiery baptism from Ray Lindwall effectively removed him from the Test team — he had been the Australian bowlers' prime target that season — but he returned to the side for the final match in the series and played two invaluable innings to help England clinch the Ashes. Some of his best Test performances came in the mid-Fifties. Against the 1956 Australians he averaged 90.60 (453 runs) for the five Tests, while captaining the side to victory in the series; a model of consistency, he was only once dismissed for less than fifty in seven innings, and that was for 43. A year later against West Indies at Edgbaston, with England trailing by 288 on the first innings, he and Colin Cowdrey put on 411 for the fourth wicket to save the match. May's contribution of 285 not out remains the highest score by an England captain. Altogether he skippered England in forty-one Tests over a period of six years, winning series against South Africa, Australia, New Zealand, India and West Indies. A shrewd captain who led from the front, and a courteous and modest man, Peter May was much liked and respected by his fellow cricketers. Illness and business commitments forced his early retirement from Test cricket at the age of 31, depriving England of one of its all-time greats.

First-class career (1948–63): 27,592 runs (51.00) including 85 centuries
Test matches (66): 4537 runs (46.77) including 13 centuries

Master batsman and gracious captain of iron will, he drove the bowlers with a relentless ferocity that was matched only by the way he drove himself.
M.C.C.

Rodger Towers

ALAN PHILIP ERIC KNOTT

b. Belvedere, Kent, 9 April 1946

Kent, Tasmania and England

Alan Knott is the third of the great trio of Kent and England wicket-keepers – Leslie Ames and Godfrey Evans are the others – and statistically the most successful. He was the first wicket-keeper to score 4000 runs in Tests, and only Australian Rodney Marsh has claimed more Test victims. Small, dark with a sharp profile reminiscent of Mr Punch, the ever-exercising Knott is an unmistakable figure behind the stumps, bending and stretching between deliveries like a puppet on a string. Unlike Evans, he prefers to stand back to the medium-pacers, his acrobatic catching in that position converting many a half-chance into a dismissal. Close to the stumps his work has been equally impressive, particularly in his long and fruitful association with county colleague Derek Underwood. As a batsman Knott has shown the same flair, judgement and determination that has characterised his performance behind the wicket. Skilful and resolute in defence yet always ready to launch an attack, his lively footwork and splendidly unorthodox strokeplay steered England through many a crisis and secured Knott's place in the side ahead of his main rival, Bob Taylor. In his first Test, against Pakistan in 1967, he snapped up seven catches. Nine years later at The Oval his stumping of West Indian Lawrence Rowe took him past Godfrey Evans' world record of 219 dismissals. There were plenty of runs too during this period, usually when they were most needed. Typical was his bustling 69 not out at Port-of-Spain against West Indies in 1967–8 which helped England to a precious 1–0 lead in the series; his match-saving 73 not out in the following Test enabling them to hang on to it. Of his five Test centuries his 106 not out at Adelaide in 1974–5, as England's batting caved in under pressure from Lillee and Walker, was perhaps the most satisfying. It was only the second hundred ever by an English wicket-keeper against Australia, the first, in 1934, having been scored by Leslie Ames. Another great man of Kent.

First-class career (1964–   ): 16,583 runs (30.09) including 17 centuries, 1213 dismissals (1090 ct, 123 st), 2 wickets (43.50)
Test matches (95): 4389 runs (32.75) including 5 centuries, 269 dismissals (250 ct, 19 st)

Mr Consistent – has he ever had an off-day?
J.C.L.

Rodger Towers

KAPIL DEV NIKHANJ

b. Chandigarh, India, 6 January 1959

Haryana, Northamptonshire and India

Indians have got used to their cricketing heroes being on the small side, but in the six-foot Kapil Dev they at last have someone to look up to. A cheerful and enthusiastic cricketer who never stops trying, he is the best pace bowler to have come out of India for many years, a carefree attacking batsman and a fine athletic fielder. He bowls at a lively fast-medium with a natural late outswinger, delivered with a well-balanced sideways-on action; and as he has shown on more than one occasion, he has the physical and mental stamina to keep going for long spells. Kapil Dev came into prominence as a 16-year-old bowler in Ranji Trophy matches, taking 6 for 39 in the first innings of his first-class début against Punjab. Selected to play against Pakistan in 1978–9, his seven wickets in the three Tests cost 60 runs each; but in the following series against the visiting West Indians he captured 17 wickets (33.00) and scored 329 runs (65.80), with a sparkling 126 not out at Delhi. Kapil Dev's presence in the side had much to do with India's success over the next three years, during which they won series against Australia, Pakistan and England. In 1979–80 he followed his 28 wickets (22.32) against Australia with a further 32 (17.68) off Pakistan – including 11 for 146 in the Madras Test – becoming the youngest player to achieve the Test double of 1000 runs and 100 wickets. Against England in 1981–2 he turned in a fine all-round performance with 22 wickets (37.95) and 318 runs (53.00), 116 of them coming off 98 balls in the last Test at Kanpur. England had their revenge against the Indian touring side a few months later, but not before Kapil Dev had treated the spectators to some exciting displays of controlled aggression with the bat. In his four Test innings, averaging 73, he hit six sixes and 40 fours, causing a few of the English bowlers to look up to him as well.

*First-class career (1975–   ): 3803 runs (28.17) including 6 centuries, 338 wickets (28.06)
†Test matches (48): 1999 runs (31.73) including 2 centuries, 189 wickets (29.93)

*Excluding 1982–3 season   †Excluding 1982–3 series v. West Indies

Born free – a completely natural player, unfettered by the chains of technique. His joyous approach to the game remains unaffected either by the state of play or the mood of his colleagues.
M.C.C.

Ivan Rose

ARTHUR ROBERT MORRIS, MBE

b. Dungog, Sydney, N.S.W., 19 January 1922

New South Wales and Australia

On his first-class début for New South Wales against Queensland in 1940, Arthur Morris scored 148 and 111. It was a sign of things to come, although it was the war that came first. Winning his first Test cap in 1946–7 against England, the left-hand opening batsman made an inauspicious start with only 28 runs in his first three innings. Then came 155 at Melbourne, and 122 and 124 not out at Adelaide. He finished the series with 503 runs at an average of 71.85. On the tour of England in 1948 he did even better. There were centuries at Lord's (105), Headingley (182) – where he and Don Bradman put on 301 as Australia raced to a remarkable victory by seven wickets, having been set 404 in 345 minutes on the final day – and The Oval (196). His 696 runs (87.00) for the series saw him top of the averages. There were other Test hundreds off India and South Africa, but in 1950–1 Morris found himself in trouble against England and in particular Alec Bedser, who dismissed him cheaply four times. His response came in the fourth Test at Adelaide with a commanding innings of 206, his highest in Tests. There was much talk of Morris being Bedser's 'rabbit', and indeed the England bowler claimed his wicket eighteen times in Test matches; but the torrent of runs that flowed from the Australian's bat in between suggests that the honours were even. Altogether he hit eight centuries off England in totalling 2080 runs at an average of just over 50; hardly the figures of a 'rabbit'. Morris had an excellent temperament for an opener, calm and patient, a sound defence and a wide range of attacking shots, especially on the leg-side. He was most impressive when facing spin, where his brilliant footwork would come into play – a feature he demonstrated against the great Gloucestershire spinning duo of Goddard and Cook in 1948 when scoring a career-best 290 on their home ground at Bristol. There as elsewhere they have good reason to remember Arthur Morris.

First-class career (1940–64): 12,614 runs (53.67) including 46 centuries, 12 wickets (49.33)
Test matches (46): 3533 runs (46.48) including 12 centuries, 2 wickets (25.00)

Despite a partiality for left-handers, I hated bowling at Arthur because his bat always appeared considerably wider than allowed and he seemed to have so much time to tuck the ball away.
T.E.B.
Unlike most current openers, he used his feet well to get into position against fast bowlers, or to go down the wicket to the spinners.
J.C.L.
Australia's greatest left-hander and the most delightful team-mate or opponent.
R.B.

Ron Wootton

HUGH JOSEPH TAYFIELD

b. Durban, Natal, 30 January 1929

Natal, Rhodesia, Transvaal and South Africa

Before starting an over, Hugh Tayfield would kiss the Springbok on his cap for luck. But the many batsmen who fell to him were more likely victims of the bowler's wiles than of any superstition. Tayfield's off-spin was a key factor of South Africa's success in the Fifties. He made his international début against Australia in 1949, and snapped up his first hundred wickets in only twenty-two Tests (his final tally of 170 is the highest for any South African). A thoughtful, naggingly accurate bowler, he relied on subtle variations of flight and pace rather than spin to deceive the batsman. His field placings were often unorthodox: a familiar ploy was to have two silly mid-ons shoulder to shoulder while leaving a large part of the off-side vacant, tempting the batsman, at his peril, to drive against the spin or to try and loft the ball over the two close fielders. In Australia in 1952–3 Tayfield took 30 wickets (28.10) in the series, including a match-winning 13 for 165 at Melbourne, the first of two occasions on which he captured thirteen wickets in a Test. He was in equally good form in England in 1955, taking 26 wickets (21.84) in the Tests and 143 wickets (15.75) during the season. Eighteen months later, at home to England, his 37 wickets (17.18) in the rubber was a record for his country. At Durban he returned second innings figures of 8 for 69, and in the next game at Johannesburg he became the only South African to have taken nine wickets in a Test innings (9 for 113; 13 for 192 in the match). It was in the Durban Test that he bowled a spell of 137 balls without conceding a run, a record for all first-class cricket. Tayfield was a brilliant fieldsman, especially to his own bowling, and at times a useful tail-end batsman. The most distinctive feature of his batting was his habit of stubbing his toe on the ground while waiting to receive the ball, which caused him to be known the cricketing world over as 'Toey'.

First-class career (1945–63): 864 wickets (21.86), 3668 runs (17.30)
Test matches (37): 170 wickets (25.91), 862 runs (16.90)

His expertise and ability to bowl to a field was a captain's dream.
R.B.
Tough, resilient, the most accurate off-spinner I ever saw.
J.C.L.

Ivan Rose

DENIS CHARLES SCOTT COMPTON, CBE

b. Hendon, Middlesex, 23 May 1918

Middlesex, Holkar and England

In the success starved years after the war it was Denis Compton more than anyone else who kept up the spirits of English cricket supporters. Whether as a dishevelled genius at the crease or a slicked-down model in a Brylcreem advertisement, he provided much needed glamour, and the public loved him for it. Batting right hand but bowling left, his brilliant and inventive strokeplay concealed a sound basic technique. His most famous shot was the sweep, though he could hook, cut and drive along with the best of them. Only his wayward running between the wickets left anything to be desired. In the long hot summer of 1947, he scored 753 runs (94.12) against the visiting South Africans; for all first-class matches that year he totalled 3816 runs (90.85), including 18 centuries – both records for a first-class season. He also captured 73 wickets (28.12) with his 'chinamen' and googlies. Against the almighty Australians his batting often took on an heroic stance. In the 1946–7 series his 459 runs (51.00) included centuries in each innings of the Adelaide Test (147 and 103 not out); and just over a year later in England he struck a magnificent 184 at Trent Bridge, after his side had trailed by 344 runs on the first innings. Then at Old Trafford, having edged a ball from Lindwall into his face and knocked himself cold, he returned, still bleeding, to the wicket to score an unbeaten 145. Compton's highest Test innings was 278 against Pakistan in 1954; his highest in any first-class game 300 in 181 minutes against N.E. Transvaal, the fastest triple century ever. During the latter stages of his career he suffered agonies from a damaged right knee – the legacy of an old football injury – which contributed to a personally disastrous tour of Australia in 1950–1. But he fought back, and appropriately made the winning hit which returned the Ashes to England two years later. In his last Test against Australia in 1956 he scored a vintage 94, despite just having had his right knee-cap removed. It was all part of the Compton magic.

First-class career (1936–64): 38,942 runs (51.85) including 123 centuries, 622 wickets (32.27)
Test matches (78): 5807 runs (50.06) including 17 centuries, 25 wickets (56.40)

Of all the cricketers I played alongside no one gave me more pleasure. An unpredictable character, always capable of doing the extraordinary; when Denis was batting well, the sun seemed to be shining out of a clear blue sky.
M.C.C.
If Roundheads and Cavaliers were evenly matched, then Hutton would be the Roundhead and Compton the Cavalier. He was far and away the best player of off-spin I ever encountered.
J.C.L.

Mike Francis

JOHN BRIAN STATHAM, CBE

b. Manchester, Lancashire, 16 June 1930

Lancashire and England

Brian Statham was always the straight man in his fast-bowling double acts with Tyson and Trueman. While they blasted away at one end with their extra yard or two of pace, he would keep the pressure on the batsman from the other end with his unrelenting accuracy. Time after time he would miss the stumps or the edge of the bat by little more than a coat of varnish, earning a reputation for being an unlucky bowler; but as his tally of 252 Test wickets proves, he had his share of successes too. Tall and lithe, 'George', as he was known in cricketing circles, had a beautiful free-flowing action. He moved the ball in both directions off the seam, keeping it straight and on a good length so that the batsman was forced to play almost every delivery. In 1951, a few months after his entry into the first-class game, he was flown to Australia to reinforce the MCC side there, making his first Test appearance against New Zealand later in the tour. Altogether he made four trips to Australia, as well as touring South Africa, India and the West Indies. His best Test bowling figures were 7 for 39 against South Africa at Lord's in 1955, and 7 for 57 against Australia at Melbourne in 1958–9. His best match analysis was 11 for 97 in the second Test against South Africa at Lord's in 1960, a series in which he captured 27 wickets (18.18). He took more than 100 wickets in a season thirteen times, ten of them in a row, and on three occasions performed the hat-trick. Twice he took fifteen wickets in a match: against Warwickshire in 1957 (8 for 34 and 7 for 55) and Leicestershire in 1964 (7 for 71 and 8 for 37). Brian Statham reserved his aggression for his bowling, never letting disappointment or enthusiasm register in a form that would give offence to anyone. His philosophy was simply expressed: 'If they miss, I hit.' The perfect line for a straight man.

First-class career (1950–68): 2260 wickets (16.36), 5424 runs (10.80)
Test matches (70): 252 wickets (24.84), 675 runs (11.44)

I always used to say about Brian Statham that I'd throw a cocktail party every time he bowled a half volley.
J.C.L.

Ivan Rose

Robert Neil Harvey, MBE

b. Fitzroy, Victoria, 8 October 1928

Victoria, New South Wales and Australia

Neil Harvey took over where Don Bradman left off. For fifteen years after 'The Don's' retirement the great left-hander was the mainstay of Australian batting, outscoring all his contemporaries and hitting 21 centuries in Tests. Of his fellow countrymen only Bradman himself and, more recently, Greg Chappell have scored more. The youngest of four cricketing brothers, all of whom played for Victoria, Harvey made his international début against India in 1947, scoring 153 at Melbourne in only his second Test. At Headingley the following year, in his maiden Test against England and still only 19, he hit a remarkably mature 112, a brilliantly aggressive knock which put Australia on the road to victory after an uncharacteristically shaky start. Once into his stride Harvey could destroy almost any bowling attack, hooking, driving and cutting with exceptional fluency and power. He was a particularly skilful batsman on difficult pitches, as he demonstrated often enough during his four tours to England. In South Africa in 1949–50 he made 660 runs (132.00) in Tests, including four centuries; three years later when the South Africans visited Australia, he kept up the good work with four more centuries in his 834 runs (92.66) for the series – the third highest Test aggregate on record. His 205 at Melbourne remained his best Test score, though he almost capped it at Kingston against West Indies in 1954–5 when he made 204. His average for that series was 108.33, his 650 runs boosted by three centuries. When the going was really tough it was often Harvey who succeeded when all around him failed. His 92 not out (out of 184) against the lethal pace of Tyson and Statham at Sydney in 1954–5 was one such innings. Another was his defiant 69 out of 140 in four and a half hours at Headingley in 1956. Harvey, who was also an accomplished baseball player, was a magnificent fielder in the covers, saving hundreds of runs in his long career to add to those he made so gloriously with the bat.

First-class career (1946–63): 21,699 runs (50.93) including 67 centuries, 30 wickets (36.86)
Test matches (79): 6149 runs (48.41) including 21 centuries, 3 wickets (40.00)

The baby in 1948. The master for the next decade.
R.B.
Despite dismissing him for a 'king pair' at Old Trafford in 1956, I rate him as the best left-hander I ever bowled at.
J.C.L.

Ivan Rose

SIR GARFIELD ST AUBRUN SOBERS

b. Bridgetown, Barbados, 28 July 1936

Barbados, Nottinghamshire, South Australia and West Indies

Gary Sobers is probably the greatest all-rounder of all time, and the most versatile cricketer the game has seen. A left-hand batsman of spectacular power, he played to perfection every shot in the book plus a few others that he improvised with his brilliant timing and footwork. As a left-arm bowler he possessed three equally effective styles: fast-medium, delivered with a textbook side-on action, orthodox spin, and unorthodox spin in the form of googlies and 'chinamen'. While close to the wicket few fieldsmen could match him. In Tests, only Boycott has scored more runs, Bradman and Gavaskar more centuries; and only Lance Gibbs, among West Indian bowlers, has taken more wickets. Sobers made his first Test appearance at 17, taking 4 for 75 against England. Four years later he broke Len Hutton's twenty-year-old record for the highest Test innings by scoring 365 not out against Pakistan at Kingston, following it up with 125 and 109 not out in the next Test. His total of 824 runs (137.33) was the first of six occasions on which he scored more than 500 in a series. As a Test captain Sobers led by example, rarely letting the responsibilities of leadership interfere with his own performance. Against England in 1966 he captained West Indies to a 3–1 victory in the rubber, his own contribution a mere 722 runs (103.14) and 20 wickets (27.25), with match-winning centuries at Old Trafford (161) and Headingley (174), and a match-saving 163 not out at Lord's. His 254 for the World XI at Melbourne in 1972 was described by Bradman as probably the best innings ever seen in Australia. Throughout his career, runs, wickets, catches and records followed each other with far from monotonous regularity. He is the only player to have completed the Australian double of 1000 runs and 50 wickets in a season (and he did it twice!), and his six sixes in an over for Nottinghamshire against Glamorgan remains a unique feat. He became Sir Garfield Sobers in 1975.

First-class career (1953–74): 28,315 runs (54.87) including 86 centuries, 1043 wickets (27.74)
Test matches (93): 8032 runs (57.78) including 26 centuries, 235 wickets (34.03)

The greatest all-rounder in cricket history; absolutely unique. One of the finest batsmen ever, a triple purpose bowler, good enough to be chosen for West Indies purely as a seamer, wrist-spinner or orthodox slow left-armer, and a superb fieldsman. There has never been a more complete cricketer.
T.E.B.

Mike Francis

ALEC VICTOR BEDSER, CBE

b. Reading, Berkshire, 4 July 1918

Surrey and England

The extent to which the giant figure of Alec Bedser towered above his contemporaries is reflected in the fact that between 1946 and 1954, when he was England's main strike bowler, he shared the opening attack with no fewer than fourteen partners. Alec and his identical twin Eric (right-hand batsman and off-spinner) made their County Championship début for Surrey in 1946. After only ten matches Alec was selected for England against India, taking 11 for 145 in his first Test and following it up with 11 for 93 in the next. That winter he toured Australia, his 16 wickets in the series including that of Don Bradman bowled for nought at Adelaide (the first of two occasions on which he dismissed the great man for a duck). Bowling off an economically short run with a perfectly balanced action, the ball despatched with a heave of his massive shoulders, Bedser was a model of accuracy, toiling away over after over without ever losing control of length or direction. Fast medium, his stock ball was the inswinger moving very late in flight, which claimed many a victim round the corner at backward short-leg. But his most destructive weapon was undoubtedly the slightly slower leg-cutter, in effect a fast leg-break, which on a rain-affected pitch especially was almost unplayable. Five times he captured 10 or more wickets in a Test, his best figures – 14 for 99 – coming against Australia at Trent Bridge in 1953. His 39 wickets (17.48) in that series was a major factor in England regaining the Ashes after nineteen years. Significantly, 104 of his one-time record number of Test wickets were taken against the powerful Australian batting sides of the post-war period, often when he was carrying the attack virtually single-handed. It is said that very early on in their careers Alec and Eric tossed a coin to decide which of the two should remain a pace bowler. Eric lost and turned to spin. But for that, England might well have had the good fortune of a Bedser at each end.

First-class career (1939–60): 1924 wickets (20.41), 5735 runs (14.51) including one century
Test matches (51): 236 wickets (24.89), 714 runs (12.75)

He had the penetration of a world-class shock bowler and the accuracy and stamina of a stock bowler. His natural delivery was the inswinger, despite a classical outswinger's action.
T.E.B.

His leg-cutter made him a dual purpose bowler; unlike other medium-pacers he would pick up wickets on slow-turners.
J.C.L.

Rodger Towers

ROHAN BABULAL KANHAI

b. Port Maurant, Guyana, 26 December 1935

Guyana, Trinidad, Warwickshire, Western Australia, Tasmania and West Indies

In the galaxy of great West Indian batsmen Rohan Kanhai is one of the brightest stars. The small right-hander from Guyana combined the Caribbean flair for extravagant strokeplay with a sound defensive technique and the temperament for playing a long Test innings. With timing and reflexes that complemented his dazzling array of attacking shots, which included a few of his own invention (it was nothing to see him sweep a ball over the ropes, only to fall flat on his back in the process), Kanhai consistently plundered runs off bowlers of every type the world over. In his first Test series in England in 1957 it was mainly promise that he showed, failing to reach 50 in any of his ten excursions to the wicket; but in India and Pakistan the following year he confirmed his potential with innings of 256 at Calcutta (still the highest score in a Test in India) and 217 off Pakistan at Lahore. In the famous 'Tied Test' series of 1960–1, he established another record when he became the first West Indian to score a hundred in each innings of a Test in Australia (117 and 115 at Adelaide). For seventeen years Kanhai was an almost permanent fixture in the West Indian side, an injury eventually ending his run of sixty-one consecutive Test appearances. His fifteen Test centuries were generously distributed: five each off England and Australia, four against India and the one double hundred in Pakistan. As Sobers' successor he proved to be a capable though somewhat contentious captain, winning one rubber and drawing another against England, but losing a series in Australia. After his departure from the Test scene in 1974 he continued to play for Warwickshire, for whom he had performed many prodigious feats with the bat since joining them six years earlier. There was time for at least one more. Against Gloucestershire in 1974 he and John Jameson created a world-record second-wicket partnership of 465 (unbroken). Rohan Kanhai's contribution was a star struck 213 not out.

*First-class career (1955–81): 28,774 runs (49.01) including
83 centuries, 18 wickets (56.05)
Test matches (79): 6227 runs (47.53) including 15 centuries*

**Spectacular, brilliant and even sounder when he got tired of
picking himself up off the floor.
J.C.L.**

Rodger Towers

IMRAN KHAN NIAZI

b. Lahore, Pakistan, 25 November 1952

Lahore, Oxford University, Worcestershire, Sussex and Pakistan

The gods have smiled on Imran Khan. As well as brains, good looks and a fine physique (not to mention family connections: he is a cousin of Majid Khan), they have bestowed on him the kind of cricketing talent not given to ordinary mortals. A bowler of genuine pace and hostility, a splendid attacking batsman and a magnificent fielder, he vies with Ian Botham and Kapil Dev for the title of Best All-Rounder in the World. With no shortage of good batsmen in the Pakistan side it is Imran's fast bowling that has been in greatest demand, and the aspect of his game that has developed most significantly over the years. He made his first Test appearance at 18 against England, but it was some time before he held a regular place in the team. His first really outstanding performance came in the third Test at Sydney in 1976–7, when with match figures of 12 for 165 he helped Pakistan to a maiden Test victory in Australia. At Lahore in 1980–1 he scored his first Test century, 123 against West Indies; and on the same ground a little more than a year later, he taught the new boys, Sri Lanka, a lesson by taking 8 for 58 (his best figures to date) and 6 for 58 in the third Test; a Pakistan record. Imran captained the touring side to England in 1982 and won the 'Man of the Series' award for his fine all-round performance in the three Tests: 212 runs (53.00) and 21 wickets (18.57). His 7 for 52 at Edgbaston is the best analysis by a Pakistan bowler in Tests against England. In the six-Test series against India in 1982–3 he managed to score 247 runs (61.75) in the few opportunities he had to bat, and captured 40 wickets (14.00), becoming the first Pakistan bowler to achieve 200 Test dismissals. At Faisalabad in the third Test his figures were 11 for 182, and for good measure he slammed the Indian attack to the blistering tune of 117. It was enough to make the gods smile.

First-class career (1969–   ): 11,534 runs (33.04) including 19 centuries, 930 wickets (22.77)

Test matches (49): 1857 runs (29.95) including 2 centuries, 232 wickets (22.93)

Excluding 1982–3 season

The Prince of princes. The modern-day Miller.
R.B.

Rodger Towers

GEOFFREY BOYCOTT, OBE

b. Fitzwilliam, Yorkshire, 21 October 1940

Yorkshire, Northern Transvaal and England

Geoffrey Boycott has had many fine summers in his career, but none more glorious than that of 1977. After a self-imposed exile of three years and thirty Tests, he returned to the English side against Australia with scores of 107 and 80 not out. Then in the very next Test, in front of his home crowd at Headingley, he notched his hundredth first-class century, thus following in the footsteps of those other great Yorkshire openers, Len Hutton and Herbert Sutcliffe. It was another memorable chapter in a cricketing story that has been full of drama, controversy and runs. Boycott's first Test appearance was against Australia in 1964; eighteen years later in India he became the world's top run-scorer in Tests, overtaking the record held by Gary Sobers. Essentially an orthodox right-hand batsman with a superb defensive technique, he relies on timing and placement rather than power to beat the field. The runs are acquired methodically with the minimum of risk, many of them square on the off-side where he is particularly strong. Only occasionally does he show any sustained aggression, as in his magnificently struck 146 in the Gillette Cup Final of 1965. He has taken centuries off all the other Test-playing countries (except Sri Lanka), the highest of them 246 not out against India in 1967, after which he was dropped for slow scoring. Without doubt one of his greatest performances was against West Indies in the final Test at Port-of-Spain in 1974, when with innings of 99 and 112 he helped win the match and square the rubber. Controversially dismissed as Yorkshire's captain in 1978 after eight years in the job, he nevertheless continued to be the county's most successful batsman, his six centuries in 1982 (at the age of 41) placing him ahead of any other Englishman in the first-class averages. Geoff Boycott's single-minded dedication to his own game has often led to accusations of selfishness. But Yorkshire and England have a lot to thank him for.

First-class career (1962–   ): 42,269 runs (56.28) including 132 centuries, 44 wickets (30.90)
Test matches (108): 8114 runs (47.72) including 22 centuries, 7 wickets (54.57)

One of the few modern cricketers who would have been considered great at any period in the history of the game.
J.C.L.

Ivan Rose

Ivan Rose 83.

RODNEY WILLIAM MARSH, MBE

b. Armadale, Perth, W.A., 4 November 1947

Western Australia and Australia

Rodney Marsh has made more Test appearances than any other Australian, yet his first might easily have been his last. A controversial selection to play against Ray Illingworth's side in 1970–1, chosen more for his batting than his wicket-keeping talent, he was dubbed 'Irongloves' by the crowd because of his fumbling of the ball. But Marsh and the selectors persevered and before long the burly, fiercely competitive character under the green cap became one of the most successful and influential members of the team. There has probably never been a better wicket-keeper to fast bowling, conveniently at a time when Australia has relied almost entirely on a pace attack. His remarkable partnership with fellow Western Australian Dennis Lillee has made 'c Marsh b Lillee' the best-known catchphrase in the game. He has been behind the stumps for every ball that Lillee has bowled in Test matches and his 89 catches off him, many of them spectacularly at full stretch, is a Test record. Marsh may inspire confidence in his own bowlers, but as a batsman he is apt to demoralise other people's. A left-hander (though right-handed in everything else), he cuts and drives with tremendous force and delights in belting the ball back over the bowler's head. He scored a hundred on his first-class début for Western Australia against the visiting West Indians in 1968. His 118 not out off Pakistan at Adelaide in 1972 was the first Test century by an Australian wicket-keeper, and his timely and unbeaten 110 in the 1977 Centenary Test the first against England. In 1981 he became the first wicket-keeper from either country to claim 100 victims in Anglo–Australian Tests, and later in the same series he passed Alan Knott's record number of Test wickets. Against England in 1982–3 he established another world record with his 28 dismissals in the series, beating the previous best total of 26 which he shared with the South African J. H. B. Waite. All things considered, dropping Rodney Marsh would have proved a costly mistake.

**First-class career (1968–   ): 9986 runs (31.70) including
10 centuries, 742 dismissals (684 ct, 58 st), 1 wicket (74.00)*
*Test matches (91): 3558 runs (26.75) including 3 centuries,
334 dismissals (322 ct, 12 st)*
*Excluding 1982–3 season

**Old 'Irongloves' finished up as pure Australian steel.
R.B.**

Rodger Towers

BARRY ANDERSON RICHARDS

b. Durban, Natal, 21 July 1945

Natal, Gloucestershire, Hampshire, South Australia and South Africa

Although Barry Richards has only played in four Test matches, no one would challenge his selection as one of the fifty post-war greats. A victim of South Africa's exclusion from official international cricket, his one Test series was against Australia in 1969–70, the young right-hand opening bat making his mark with centuries at Durban (140) and Port Elizabeth (126), failing by just four deliveries to score his maiden Test hundred before lunch. It is part of Richards' genius that he makes batting look so easy. An excellent judge of line and length, he appears to have masses of time in which to play his many shots, striking the ball with the full face of the bat. Equally strong on the front or back foot, his strokeplay is an exciting combination of elegance and power. If he has a weakness it is perhaps one of temperament, a tendency to become bored and careless if his supreme skills are not fully tested by the opposition. As an occasional off-spinner he has also had his moments of glory, in one match against the Rest of the World in 1968 returning the highly respectable figures of 7 for 63. Deprived of Test cricket, Richards has divided his time and talent between the domestic competitions of England, Australia and South Africa. For Hampshire in the 1970s his spectacular run-happy opening partnerships with West Indian Gordon Greenidge made a mockery of apartheid and of much of the bowling they faced. Nine times he scored more than 1000 runs in a season, and twice made a century in each innings of a match (v. Northants in 1968 and Kent in 1976). Playing for South Australia in 1970–1, he was even more prolific. His total of 1538 runs (109.85) included an innings of 224 off the MCC touring side, with another of 146 coming in a second match against them. His highest score was a career-best 356 against Western Australia, 325 of them in a single day. That season Richards cost his sponsors a dollar a run. But his loss to Test cricket is incalculable.

*First-class career (1964–   ): 27,768 runs (55.31) including 79 centuries, 77 wickets (37.38)
Test matches (4): 508 runs (72.57) including 2 centuries, 1 wicket (26.00)
*Excluding 1982–3 season

Technically the most perfect batsman I have seen, straight out of a coaching manual. Missed the challenge of international cricket, so that he sometimes gave the impression of being interested in batting, but not the game.
T.E.B.
No more elegant player has taken the field in our time.
R.B.

Mike Francis

ALAN KEITH DAVIDSON, OBE

b. Lisarow, Nr Gosford, N.S.W., 14 June 1929

New South Wales and Australia

All-rounder Alan Davidson could almost take his place among the '50 Greatest' on the basis of his fielding alone. His legendary catching close to the wicket won him the nickname 'The Claw', and he was equally brilliant in the outfield. With his hostile bowling, aggressive batting and dynamic fielding, he epitomised the hard Australian approach to the game. Although not as fast as Lindwall or Lillee or even McKenzie, his left-arm fast-medium bowling was menacing enough. He moved the new ball very late in the air, and off the pitch in either direction. His normal delivery was angled across the right-hander from over the wicket, but every so often he would nip one back into the batsman. Against England in 1958–9, when Australia trounced what appeared on paper to be an exceptionally strong side 4–0, Davidson was the main strike bowler with 24 wickets (19.00) in the series. In the third over of the Melbourne Test he knocked the stuffing out of England's batting by taking their first three wickets in five balls, finishing with 6 for 64. He repeated his success against England in 1961 and 1962–3, picking up a further 47 wickets; but his most successful series with the ball was against West Indies in 1960–1. Playing in only four of the five Tests, he captured 33 wickets (18.54) and took five or more in an innings in every game. With his invaluable all-round contribution in the famous tied match at Brisbane (11 for 222, and innings of 44 and 80), he became the first player to take 10 wickets and score 100 runs in a Test. Usually batting at No. 7 or 8, his pugnacious hitting could swing a match in a matter of a few overs – as it did at Old Trafford in 1961, when his unbeaten 77 (and a last-wicket partnership of 98 with McKenzie) helped to turn impending defeat into a remarkable victory for the Australians. One way or another, Alan Davidson was a hard man to ignore.

First-class career (1949–63): 6804 runs (32.86) including 9 centuries, 672 wickets (20.90)
Test matches (44): 1328 runs (24.59), 186 wickets (20.53)

When he learned to swing the ball into the right-hand batsman from outside the off stump, he became for several seasons the most feared opening bowler in the world. In addition, he was a rumbustious batsman and an exceptional fielder, especially 'round the corner'.
T.E.B.
One of the greatest all-round cricketers to grace the game.
R.B.

Rodger Towers

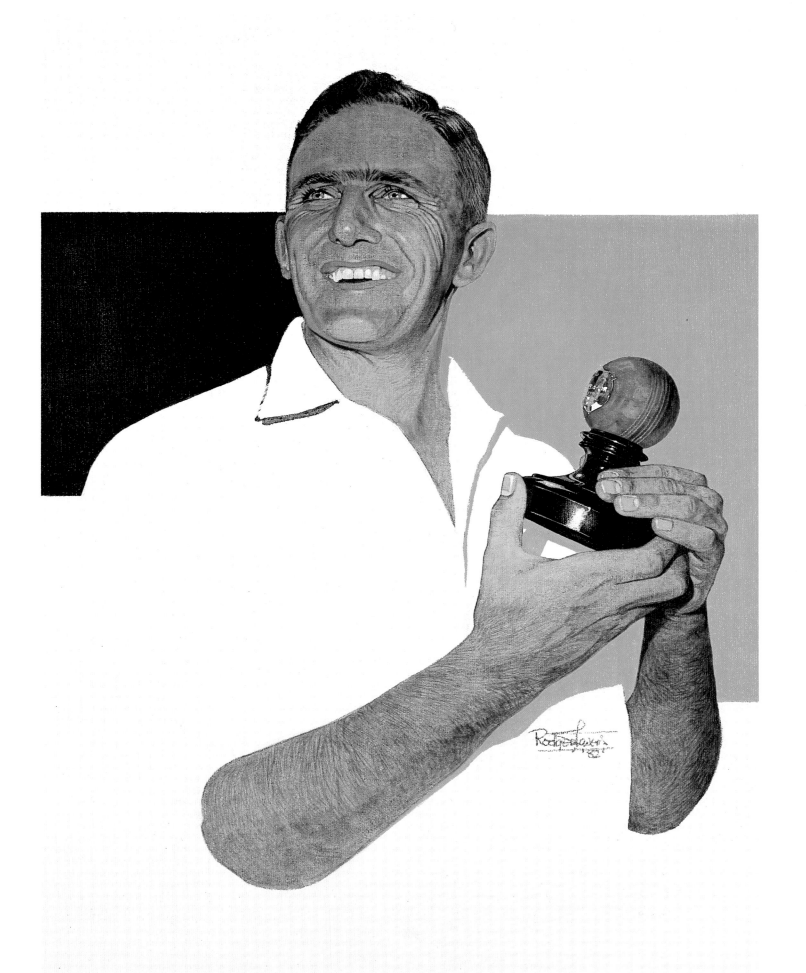

CLIVE HUBERT LLOYD

b. Georgetown, Guyana, 31 August 1944

Guyana, Lancashire and West Indies

The tall, gangling, bespectacled figure of Clive Lloyd hardly fits the cliché image of a cricketing superstar. Few players, though, in the history of the game have hit the ball as hard as this popular left-hander from Guyana, or performed with such athletic brilliance in the field. Making full use of his long reach as he lays about him with an extra weighty bat, Lloyd can bring almost any bowling attack to its knees in a handful of overs. He cuts, hooks and drives with unrestrained ferocity, pouncing on any ball that strays off line or length. When patrolling the covers his magnetic pick-up and laser-like return have resulted in many a spectacular run out; more recently, with knee trouble forcing him to take refuge in the slips, he has pulled off some acrobatic catches close to the wicket. In the early days he was also a useful right-arm medium-pace bowler. He made an impressive start to his Test career in 1966–7 with innings of 82 and 78 not out at Bombay. Centuries against England and Australia followed; then, in 1974–5, he took over the captaincy from Rohan Kanhai, starting as he clearly meant to continue with 163 (the first 100 off 85 balls) in the first Test against India at Bangalore. In the last match of the series, which West Indies won 3–2, he struck a magnificent 242 not out. Under his leadership West Indies took the first Prudential World Cup in 1975 (and the second in 1979), Lloyd himself contributing a match-winning 102 in the final. Then, the celebrations barely over, came a crushing 5–1 defeat at the hands of Australia 'down under', and suddenly his future as captain seemed in doubt. But with victories in quick succession against India, England and Pakistan, Lloyd and Co. were soon back in business, and he now holds the world record for the most Tests as captain. As for Lancashire, where he has given such great value over the years, Clive Lloyd's image could hardly be better.

*First-class career (1964–   ): 27,334 runs (48.98) including 70 centuries, 114 wickets (36.00)
†Test matches (85): 5831 runs (43.84) including 14 centuries, 10 wickets (62.20)

*Excluding 1982–3 season   †Excluding 1982–3 series v. India

Doesn't waste an inch of his physique, especially in the field. The modern West Indian answer to Learie Constantine. J.C.L.

Rodger Towers

JOEL GARNER

b. in Barbados, 16 December 1952

Barbados, Somerset, South Australia and West Indies

Ask any Somerset supporter what their favourite bird is and the chances are they will answer 'Joel Garner'. The six-foot-eight-inch Barbadian, known to everyone as 'Big Bird', has won many West Country hearts and not a few matches since joining the county in 1977. A right-arm fast-medium bowler, operating off a relatively short run, Garner maintains immaculate control of line and length. He can move the ball either way and uses his exceptional height to gain extra bounce, causing most batsmen no end of problems. Accurately pitching the ball just short of a length, he is extremely difficult to score off, which makes him an invaluable asset in limited-overs cricket. In Test matches, as one of a battery of West Indian pace men, he has tended to come on as first or second change after others have launched the initial assault with the new ball, but has been no less dangerous for that. He arrived on the Test scene in 1976–7, capturing 25 wickets (27.52) in the five-match series at home against Pakistan. The following year, after taking 13 wickets in the first two Tests against Australia, he withdrew from the side along with other World Series cricketers. Back in the West Indian team for the Prudential World Cup final against England in 1979, his 5 for 38 (four of them clean bowled) made certain that the trophy stayed in the Caribbean. He was still a thorn in England's flesh a year later, heading the averages with 26 wickets (14.26) in the five-Test rubber, which West Indies won 1–0. Garner's best Test bowling figures to date are 6 for 56 against New Zealand at Auckland in 1980; and in all first-class matches 8 for 31 for Somerset v. Glamorgan in 1977. As a tail-ender with the longest reach in the game he has played several useful innings, including one of 104 for the West Indians against Gloucestershire in 1980. An easy figure to spot wherever he is in the field, the 'Big Bird' from Barbados is a welcome visitor every summer.

*First-class career (1976–   ): 490 wickets (17.32), 1605 runs (17.44) including one century
†Test matches (28): 124 wickets (20.64), 400 runs (11.76)

*Excluding 1982–3 season   †Excluding 1982–3 series v. India

Cricket's most unusual giant has set problems of steepness and bounce for the batsmen which they have never had to face before. Fortunately for those on the receiving end, there is no malice in him.
M.C.C.

Ivan Rose

GLENN MAITLAND TURNER

b. Dunedin, New Zealand, 26 May 1947

Otago, Worcestershire and New Zealand

In 1967 Warwickshire, their quota of overseas players already filled, recommended a young New Zealand opener to neighbouring Worcestershire. Over the next fifteen years Glenn Turner became the county's most outstanding batsman, scoring no less than 72 centuries, ten of them in 1970, a club record. In between times, in keeping with the jet-setting lifestyle of the modern cricketer, he has performed great deeds for New Zealand and his native Otago. Turner is a dedicated professional, his trim figure concealing a gargantuan appetite for runs. The masterly defensive technique and ability to play a long pains-taking innings were evident early on, but it was some years before the wraps came off his impressive range of attacking shots. A predictably good judge of line and length, he plays immaculately straight and is a fine driver of the ball both sides of the wicket. In 1973, as a member of the New Zealand touring team, he joined that élite group who have scored more than 1000 runs before the end of May (1018: average 78.30). Twice in Tests he has carried his bat through an entire innings: against England – and in particular Derek Underwood – at Lord's in 1969 with 43 out of 131; and at Sabina Park against West Indies, scoring 223 out of a total of 386 (later in the series he established another New Zealand Test record with his innings of 259 at Georgetown). He has made two centuries in a match on six occasions, most notably at Christchurch in 1974 where his 101 and 110 not out helped New Zealand to beat Australia for the first time in a Test. He has captained his country ten times, but disagreements with the administrators have reduced his number of appearances for New Zealand in recent years. Before taking leave of Worcestershire in 1982, Glenn Turner recorded his hundredth first-class century and hit a career-best 311 not out off Warwickshire. It was the first triple century in a day in England for thirty-three years, and a painful reminder to his original sponsors of what they had missed.

*First-class career (1964–   ): 34,213 runs (49.87) including 103 centuries, 5 wickets (37.80)
Test matches (41): 2991 runs (44.64) including 7 centuries
*Excluding 1982–3 season

From a fragile and seemingly commonplace acorn came an oak of remarkable stature and power.
M.C.C.

Mike Francis

BISHAN SINGH BEDI

b. Amritsar, India, 25 September 1946

Punjab, Delhi, Northamptonshire and India

There have been few greater pleasures in the modern game than watching Bishan Bedi bowl. Full of Eastern guile and artistry, his gentle approach to the wicket and graceful movement of the arm cunningly concealed the aggression in his bowling. At his peak, Bedi's slow left-arm spin troubled most of the world's leading batsmen, deceiving them through the air with his curving flight or beating them off the pitch with subtle changes of pace and turn. His beautifully relaxed and co-ordinated action enabled him to bowl all day if required without losing rhythm or control, and his stamina and patience seemed inexhaustible. He made his first-class début for Northern Punjab in the Ranji Trophy at the remarkably young age of 15; even more remarkably he had taken up cricket only two years before. He arrived on the Test scene in 1966, selected to play against West Indies at Calcutta, and despite healthy competition from his fellow Indian spinners has taken more wickets for his country than any other bowler. On two occasions against England he captured 25 wickets in a series (1972–3 and 1976–7); and the five Tests in Australia in 1977–8 brought him 31 wickets (23.87), including match figures of 10 for 194 at Perth. He achieved an even better strike rate against New Zealand in 1976–7 with 22 wickets (13.18) in three Tests. Bedi captained India in twenty-two Test matches between 1976 and 1978, in six of them to victory. His best bowling figures in first-class cricket were 7 for 5 (13 for 34 in the match) for Delhi against Jammu and Kashmir in 1974–5; his best in Tests 7 for 98 against Australia at Calcutta in 1969–70. English spectators were privileged to see a lot of Bishan Bedi in the Seventies during his six-year spell with Northamptonshire. He twice took 100 wickets in a season for the county, and successfully demonstrated that slow bowlers can be a force in the limited-overs game. A popular figure wherever he played, the Sikh from Amritsar brought to cricket his own inimitable style and a natty line in patkas.

First-class career (1961–81): 1560 wickets (21.69), 3584 runs (11.37)
Test matches (67): 266 wickets (28.71), 656 runs (8.98)

My dream match would be to see Bishan Bedi at one end and Ray Lindwall at the other.
J.C.L.

Mike Francis

EDWARD RALPH DEXTER

b. Milan, Italy, 15 May 1935

Cambridge University, Sussex and England

Ted Dexter was one of the most glamorous sporting figures of the Sixties. Known throughout the cricketing world as 'Lord Ted', he was an extravagantly gifted player with an adventurous spirit that couldn't resist a challenge. A stylish and fearless batsman, he believed in carrying the attack to even the fastest bowlers, driving with great power off the front and back foot. His own bowling was a lively medium-pace with lots of swing, particularly in English conditions, though as time went on he was used mainly as a change bowler. It was with the ball that he made his mark in representative cricket, taking 5 for 8 and 3 for 47 in the 1957 Gentlemen v. Players match. The following year he made his first Test appearance against New Zealand, and secured his place in the English side during the 1959–60 tour of the West Indies by scoring two Test hundreds and finishing top of the averages. There have been few more regal sights on a cricket field than E. R. Dexter in full flow. No one who saw it will forget his spectacular 76 in 84 minutes against Richie Benaud's Australians at Old Trafford in 1961; or his daring counter-attack on Hall and Griffiths at Lord's in 1963, when he hammered 70 in 81 glorious minutes. In a different vein were his two marathon match-saving innings against Australia: 180 at Edgbaston in 1961, and 174 in eight hours at Old Trafford in 1964. His highest Test score was 205 against Pakistan at Karachi in 1961–2; his best bowling figures, also against Pakistan, 4 for 10 at Headingley in 1962. He led England in thirty Tests between 1961–4 with qualified success, stepping down from the captaincy to stand for Parliament. To no one's surprise – since his opponent was James Callaghan – he failed to win the seat and returned to the serious business of Test cricket. Four years later, and far too soon, 'Lord Ted' left the game to his peers.

First-class career (1956–70): 21,150 runs (40.75) including 51 centuries, 419 wickets (29.92)
Test matches (62): 4502 runs (47.89) including 9 centuries, 66 wickets (34.93)

The most gifted all-round English cricketer since Hammond, he produced one or two of the best innings by an Englishman post-war. But he derived more pleasure from the pursuit of perfection than in its accomplishment.
M.C.C.

Ron Wootton

GRAHAM DOUGLAS McKENZIE

b. Cottesloe, Perth, W.A., 24 June 1941

Western Australia, Leicestershire and Australia

Over six feet tall, broad-shouldered and weighing in at fourteen and a half stones, Graham McKenzie was nicknamed 'Garth' by his team-mates after the giant strong man in a strip cartoon. He had the perfect build for a fast bowler, and made the most of it. Moving in easily along an economical run-up, he saved his strength for the moment of delivery, slamming the ball into the ground so that it lifted sharply off a length. He was not a great swinger of the ball, but moved it appreciably off the seam away from the right-hander. McKenzie more or less bridged the gap between Lindwall and Lillie, although he was not as fast as either of them. He burst on to the Test scene at Lord's in 1961 – on his twentieth birthday – taking a match-winning 5 for 37 in England's second innings, after having earlier scored an invaluable 34 runs batting at number ten. Between December 1963 and December 1964 he set up a new record of 73 Test wickets in a calendar year: 16 against South Africa, 29 against England, and 28 against India and Pakistan; his 29 wickets in England equalling Clarrie Grimmett's long-standing record for an Australian bowler in the 'Old Country'. At 23, he became the youngest-ever bowler to take 100 wickets in Tests, and four years later the youngest to reach the 200 mark. His best Test figures were 8 for 71 against West Indies at Melbourne in 1968. Other outstanding performances include his 7 for 153 at Old Trafford in 1964 as England compiled a massive 611; match figures of 10 for 91 against India at Madras in 1964–5; and 6 for 48 in England's first innings at Adelaide in 1966. Towards the end of his Test career McKenzie, who had spearheaded his country's attack for almost ten years, showed understandable signs of exhaustion; but he continued to play county cricket for Leicestershire until the mid-Seventies. A quiet, modest and easy-going character, 'Garth' was of the gentle species of giant. Except, of course, when bowling.

First-class career (1959–75): 1218 wickets (26.98), 5662 runs (15.59)
Test matches (60): 246 wickets (29.78), 945 runs (12.27)

'Garth', the gentle giant who carried the Australian bowling attack for most of his career.
R.B.

Ron Wootton

SYED ZAHEER ABBAS

b. Sialkot, Pakistan, 24 July 1947

Pakistan International Airlines, Karachi, Gloucestershire and Pakistan

If there are any drawbacks to wearing glasses Zaheer Abbas clearly doesn't see them. The bespectacled Pakistani is one of the most attractive and prolific batsmen in the game today, a deceptively casual stroke-maker with a flowing, loose-wristed style that sends the ball racing to the boundary time and again. Once into his stride he is seldom restricted by either the bowlers or the wicket, treating the spectators to an exhilarating display of grace, skill and power. In 1971 at Edgbaston, in only his second Test match and his first against England, he scored 274 in a remarkable innings which lasted nine hours four minutes. Three years later at The Oval there was almost an action replay of the event with another giant knock of 240 in the third Test. But then Zaheer Abbas has a habit of repeating himself. Since joining Gloucestershire in 1972, he has scored 1000 runs in an English season ten times and on four occasions – a world record – has hit a double and a single hundred in the same match, astonishingly without losing his wicket once in the process (altogether he has performed the feat of two separate hundreds in the same game eight times, beating Wally Hammond's long-standing record). In 1981 he achieved the equivalent of 'a thousand runs in May' by scoring 1016 in June, not having played at all before that, and finished top of the first-class averages that season with 2306 runs (88.69) including ten centuries. He had a disappointing series for Pakistan against England in 1982, but made up for it with a vengeance when his side met India a few months later. In the first three Tests, batting only once in each, his scores were 215, 186 and 168. He finished the series with 650 runs to his credit, at an average of 130. During the course of this scoring spree, he became the first Pakistan batsman to reach 4000 runs in Tests and only the third player from outside England to have made 100 first-class centuries (the others are Don Bradman and Glenn Turner); proving that with Zaheer, it is usually the bowlers who have the handicap.

*First-class career (1966–   ): 30,069 runs (52.84) including 95 centuries, 25 wickets (33.12)
Test matches (58): 4073 runs (46.81) including 11 centuries
*Excluding 1982–3 season

How good would this magnificent batsman have been with 20/20 vision?
R.B.

Glasses have been no hindrance to him. His ability to 'sight' the line and length of the ball have made him one of the most fluent drivers in the business.
J.C.L.

Rodger Towers

THE 50 GREATEST BY COUNTRY

ENGLAND

KEN BARRINGTON
ALEC BEDSER
IAN BOTHAM
GEOFFREY BOYCOTT
DENIS COMPTON
TED DEXTER
GODFREY EVANS
LEN HUTTON
ALAN KNOTT
PETER MAY
BRIAN STATHAM
FRED TRUEMAN
DEREK UNDERWOOD

WEST INDIES

JOEL GARNER
LANCE GIBBS
WESLEY HALL
ROHAN KANHAI
CLIVE LLOYD
VIVIAN RICHARDS
ANDY ROBERTS
GARFIELD SOBERS
CLYDE WALCOTT
EVERTON WEEKES
FRANK WORRELL

NEW ZEALAND

RICHARD HADLEE
BERT SUTCLIFFE
GLENN TURNER

AUSTRALIA

DON BRADMAN
GREG CHAPPELL
IAN CHAPPELL
ALAN DAVIDSON
WALLY GROUT
NEIL HARVEY
DENNIS LILLEE
RAY LINDWALL
GRAHAM MCKENZIE
RODNEY MARSH
KEITH MILLER
ARTHUR MORRIS

SOUTH AFRICA

GRAEME POLLOCK
MIKE PROCTER
BARRY RICHARDS
HUGH TAYFIELD

INDIA

BISHAN BEDI
SUNIL GAVASKAR
KAPIL DEV
'VINOO' MANKAD

PAKISTAN

HANIF MOHAMMAD
IMRAN KHAN
ZAHEER ABBAS

THE 50 GREATEST BY CATEGORY

OPENING BATSMEN

GEOFFREY BOYCOTT
SUNIL GAVASKAR
HANIF MOHAMMAD
LEN HUTTON
ARTHUR MORRIS
BERT SUTCLIFFE
GLENN TURNER

OTHER BATSMEN

KEN BARRINGTON
DON BRADMAN
GREG CHAPPELL
IAN CHAPPELL
DENIS COMPTON
TED DEXTER
NEIL HARVEY
ROHAN KANHAI
CLIVE LLOYD
PETER MAY
GRAEME POLLOCK
BARRY RICHARDS
VIVIAN RICHARDS
CLYDE WALCOTT
EVERTON WEEKES
FRANK WORRELL
ZAHEER ABBAS

PACE BOWLERS

ALEC BEDSER
JOEL GARNER

WESLEY HALL
DENNIS LILLEE
RAY LINDWALL
GRAHAM MCKENZIE
ANDY ROBERTS
BRIAN STATHAM
FRED TRUEMAN

SPIN BOWLERS

BISHAN BEDI
LANCE GIBBS
HUGH TAYFIELD
DEREK UNDERWOOD

ALL-ROUNDERS

IAN BOTHAM
ALAN DAVIDSON
RICHARD HADLEE
IMRAN KHAN
KAPIL DEV
'VINOO' MANKAD
KEITH MILLER
MIKE PROCTER
GARFIELD SOBERS

WICKET-KEEPERS

GODFREY EVANS
WALLY GROUT
ALAN KNOTT
RODNEY MARSH

THE CONTRIBUTORS

Mike Francis' work has been regularly exhibited in London (at the Nicholas Treadwell Gallery) and in various collections throughout Europe and the USA. He lives and works in Sidcup, Kent, and his interests apart from painting include photography, football and cricket. His grandfather, who taught him how to bowl, played occasionally for Sussex alongside two of the greatest names from the 'Golden Age', K. S. Ranjitsinhji and C. B. Fry.

Ivan Rose began work at 15 as a model maker and served his apprenticeship with Rank Screen Advertising. Since then he has been a freelance artist and illustrator, lecturing from time to time at art schools in London and Perth. He lives now in Middlesex and his past sporting activities include fencing for Wembley and rowing for Twickenham. When he is not flexing his muscles, he likes to collect antiques.

Rodger Towers worked for ten years in London advertising agencies as a visualiser/typographer before going freelance in 1967. He spent six years designing record sleeves for EMI, then broadened out into other areas of illustration. Since then his work has been featured in scores of advertisements, and on countless film posters and book jackets. He is a keen amateur yachtsman and a supporter of Surrey County Cricket Club.

Ron Wootton spent his national service as the battalion artist. Back in civvy street he joined a leading London advertising agency as a visualiser/illustrator, and later became Creative Head of the department. He went freelance as an illustrator in 1967, and now has a studio in London and at his home in Kent. His favourite pastimes are sailing, listening to classical music and painting watercolour landscapes, which he sells from his home gallery in Kent as well as having them on show in local exhibitions.

Since collaborating on *The Fifty Greatest*, Mike Francis, Ivan Rose, Rodger Towers and Ron Wootton have formed a design and illustration partnership under the banner 'Four Artists'.

Graham Tarrant has written and edited a number of books, among them *County Champions*, a cricketing anthology published in 1982. He has also devised several television programmes, including two panel games and a dramatised documentary about a famous murder, *Who Killed Julia Wallace?* As a lifetime cricket lover he has watched Test matches in England, Australia, New Zealand, India and the West Indies. His formative years were divided between England and New Zealand, allowing him the luxury of a cricketing hero in each hemisphere : Peter May and Bert Sutcliffe. Both, he is relieved to see, have made it into *The Fifty Greatest*.

Bill Frindall is cricket's best-known statistician. Appropriately, he was born on the first day of the 'Timeless Test' played at Durban in 1939, and was eleven days old when it ended in a draw. In 1966, after six years in the RAF, he became a full-time cricket statistician and joined the BBC's Test Match Special team – since when he has had an uninterrupted run in the commentary box, covering every home Test match as well as a further twenty overseas. A grand total of more than 100 Tests. Among the books he has produced are *The Wisden Book of Test Cricket 1876–77 to 1977–78* (a second volume up to the end of the 1983 English season is to be published in 1984), *The Wisden Book of Cricket Records* and *The Guinness Book of Cricket Facts and Feats*. He is also the compiler of *The Daily Telegraph Cricket Year Book*.